C000258074

in bloom

MODERN FLORALS FOR THE HOME

in bloom

MODERN FLORALS FOR THE HOME

ALICE WHATELY

For Rollo and Francis, with love

First published in 2005 by Conran Octopus Limited
a part of Octopus Publishing Group
2–4 Heron Quays, London E14 4JP
www.conran-octopus.co.uk

Text copyright © Conran Octopus 2005
Book design and layout copyright © Conran
Octopus 2005

All rights reserved. No part of this book may be
reproduced, stored in a retrieval system, or
transmitted, in any form or by any means,
electronic, electrostatic, magnetic tape, mechanical,
photocopying, recording or otherwise, without the
prior permission in writing of the Publisher.

The right of Alice Whately to be identified as
the Author of this Work has been asserted by her
in accordance with the Copyright, Designs and
Patents Act 1988.

British Library Cataloguing-in-Publication Data.
A catalogue record for this book is available from
the British Library.

ISBN 1 84091 422 X
Printed in China

Publishing Director: Lorraine Dickey
Art Director: Chi Lam
Executive Editor: Zia Mattocks
Designer: Victoria Burley
Editor: Sian Parkhouse
Picture Research Manager: Liz Boyd
Picture Researcher: Vivien Hamley
Production Manager: Angela Couchman

contents

introduction

Floral decoration has been a popular choice in Western interiors since the seventeenth century, when chintz was first imported to Britain from the East Indies. Featuring botanical motifs in dazzling hues, the revolutionary new fabric was an instant hit – its shiny, dust-repellent finish making it a natural choice for a range of soft furnishings.

The pre-eminence of chintz during the 1700s prompted English and French textile manufacturers to develop their own versions of the fabric. Featuring a riot of cottage-garden blooms, including roses, daisies, sweet peas, carnations and tulips, the new-look chintz was later exported to America, where it was received with gusto.

These days, our desire to introduce a botanical theme to our interiors goes hand in hand with the enduring fashion for minimalism. As a result, floral decoration provides a tasteful complement to simply painted walls, wooden floors and streamlined furnishings, helping to create design schemes that are as appealing as they are contemporary.

The resurgence of floral décor has resulted in a variety of different furnishing styles – the most significant of which are examined in this book. Designed to suit a range of interiors, *In Bloom* begins with a look at Feminine Florals, in which romantic rooms are created through the introduction of pastel colours, blowsy motifs and floaty drapes. The faded furnishings that characterize a relaxed, pared-back style are also included in this chapter, in a bid to celebrate the timeworn appeal of flaky painted furniture, sun-bleached fabrics and floral slipcovers.

By contrast, decorating with Exotic Florals imbues interiors with a sense of global sophistication. Motifs, including stylized

OPPOSITE Decorative floral touches, together with an ornately carved bed, breathe life into this essentially minimalist boudoir, creating a sense of feminine sophistication.

Indian roses and Chinese lotus blossoms, are depicted in jewel-bright shades, while the fashion for glamorous Asian-style furnishings witnesses the incorporation of Chinese wallpaper, ambient lighting and exquisitely embroidered silks. Choosing to kit out your home with a variety of different global elements is also popular with contemporary homeowners, resulting in a relaxed, eclectic feel.

The Funky Floral look is characterized by graphic plants and stylized flowers that are as flash as they are funky. Offering a radical departure from traditional designs, key elements include digitalized wallpaper, modern artworks, vivid colours and jolly bead curtains. The look also encompasses fabrics and furnishings by contemporary fashion designers such as Jasper Conran, Matthew Williamson and Donna Karan.

Currently enjoying a renaissance, Retro Florals provide an appealing complement to the sleek lines of contemporary interiors. Botanical designs from the sixties and seventies jazz up stripped wooden floors and neutral-coloured walls, while the demand for flashback furnishings has resulted in a growing number of outlets selling vintage collectibles. In addition, a number of companies are now reissuing classic furniture designs, while mid-century fabrics by Marimekko are also enjoying a revival.

Perfect for traditionalists, the faded charm of Vintage Florals recalls the cosy innocence of bygone days. Featuring furnishings and fabrics that have been sourced from antique fairs and junk shops, its mix-and-match approach results in design schemes that are as original as they are inspired. Old-fashioned fabrics such as patchwork, lace and velvet are essential to the success of this look, while modern rustic-style furnishings help to compound the sense of nostalgia.

OPPOSITE Mixing floral wallpaper with modern furnishings creates a wonderfully eclectic feel, while the striped curtains compound the mix-and-match approach.

feminine florals

Flowers and floral designs are among the world's best-loved patterns, but such popularity has, on occasion, been their downfall. Certainly, florals did themselves few favours in the 1980s when they were combined with sumptuous swags and fussy frills, but now that the frou-frou flounces of yesteryear have been rigorously edited, it's a different story.

The new-look floral presents a marked departure from the previous glut of ponderous patterns and lumpen textures. Light and bright, rather than rambling and overblown, the focus is on colour, contrast and simplicity, which, combined with simply painted walls and pared-back furniture, allow the intrinsic charm of petal prints to shine through.

Today's feminine florals work as effectively in traditional interiors as they do in more contemporary ones – with the looks including **NEW ROMANTIC** and **SIMPLE CHIC**. Although these decorating schemes work well in any room in the house, they are best suited to **BEDROOMS**, **BATHROOMS**, **LIVING ROOMS** and **EATING AREAS**.

petal palette

In order to prime your home for a floral decorative scheme, it's important to first simplify your surroundings. While you may have chosen to eschew minimalism in favour of a more florid approach, this doesn't mean that clean white spaces need to go out the window. Instead, it's possible to combine elements of the two looks so that you create a home that is cool and contemporary rather than cluttered and claustrophobic.

The theory of space-clearing combines the physical process of removing any unnecessary clutter with the aesthetic one of simplifying your surroundings. Ensuring that your space is light and bright will allow blooms to breathe – a vital part of creating an attractive floral scheme. Remember: clarity is key to success.

Choosing a pale colour palette is instrumental in this process. For example, if you opt for white or off-white walls, you will create a blank canvas with beautifully classic foundations. In addition, neutral wall treatments complement a vast choice of colours, tones and textures, as well as providing a stylish backdrop for different furniture styles and floral treatments. Better still, walls that are painted in pale shades reflect natural light, automatically making your space seem bigger and brighter. But avoid too-stark whites, opting for the softer shades of string, bone, ivory and calico instead.

Keeping your flooring simple is another way of allowing floral designs to take centre stage. Instead of carpet, choose stripped wooden boards, sisal matting or sandblasted cement, which will all help to clear the decks for botanical wallpapers, upholstery and stencilled motifs – as well as providing a perfect foil for pretty Aubusson rugs.

The sensitive harnessing of light is also important. The best illumination for a bowery of feminine florals is daylight, a natural phenomenon that should be fully exploited.

COLOURS FROM THE GARDEN

Colours from the garden are a prime inspiration in the floral home:

❋ Rose red
Shades of scarlet, crimson, magenta and cerise are perennially popular, thanks to the enduring appeal of the rose. Combine with cream, pink and green for an English country-house feel, or with white for a contemporary effect.

❋ Sunflower yellow
Yellow will help to energize a room that's deprived of natural light. Team it with white to maximize the sunny feel, or with green and white to create feelings of revitalization.

❋ Delphinium blue
Said to trigger 11 tranquillizing hormones, blue is perfect for blissed-out bedrooms. Mix with violet and lilac to create the ultimate chill-out zone.

❋ Peony pink
Pink represents the fragility of love and romance. Combine with red to create an electrifying effect, or with pastel shades for a more peaceful note.

❋ Parma violet
Excellent for creating a sense of nurturing, violet soothes body, mind and spirit. Mix with white, cream or pink to compound the feminine feel, or with blues for a more laid-back vibe.

❋ Carnation white
Crisp and clean, white is the ideal backdrop for spriggy schemes. Use to make small, light-deprived rooms feel more spacious, or to create pristine bathrooms.

❋ Creamy magnolia
Soft and sensual, magnolia is perfect for sensual decorating schemes, and is frequently used to complement bold patterns and colours.

OPPOSITE An all-white décor provides a pristine setting for floral furnishings such as this elegantly upholstered sofa.

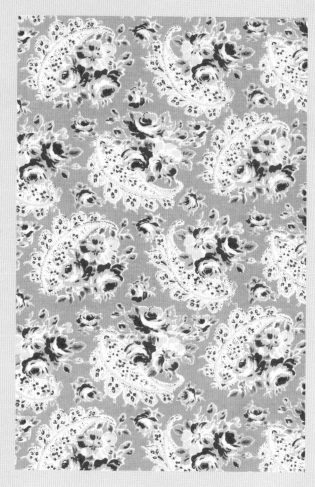

new romantic

Introducing feminine florals to your interior is one of the best ways to create a dreamy sense of romanticism. Fabrics such as floaty rose-printed drapes or silk sheets embroidered with teeny buds give a sweetly seductive look, while pastel colours such as pink, lilac and powder blue compound the sense of feminine allure. Fixtures and fittings in the shape of floral candelabras and decorative mirrors are also key in romantic room sets, together with lush linens and softly curved furniture. In terms of decorative details, opt for a few carefully chosen mementoes, including floral watercolours, scented candles and delicate blooms in single-stem vases.

LEFT These two cotton fabrics are ideal for decorative details such as cushion covers, chair seats or tablecloths; the rosebud print is a particularly good choice for new romantic boudoirs. OPPOSITE This ultra-feminine living room retains a light, airy feel with white-painted floorboards and cotton drapes in different-scale floral prints dressing the floor-to-ceiling windows. The pink sofa with scatter cushions in shades of lilac, pink and purple add blocks of colour and prevent the room from looking twee.

contemporary cutouts

One of the quickest and easiest ways to
introduce florals to the home is through the
application of stencilled motifs. A far cry from
the fuddy-duddy designs that decorated walls
during the 1980s, the new-look stencils are
cleaner, crisper and much more dramatic.

There are numerous advantages to
stencilling – the most obvious being that it
requires no greater skill than a steady hand
to convey the impression of a pattern that's
been professionally applied. There's also a
fabulous range of pre-cut stencils available –
with botanical designs ranging from Japanese
cherry blossom to wisteria, roses and daisies.

For a simple but striking look, stencil
a graphic design on a neutral backdrop;
alternatively, create maximum impact by
covering an entire wall with an intricate
pattern in a pale colour, emphasizing random
motifs in a stronger shade. Contemporary
cutouts are best suited to rooms that are big
enough to cater for modern motifs, many of
which have been designed to unfold in a fluid
continuum across walls, floors and doors.
Stencils can also be used to improve a room's
proportions, or cleverly draw attention to
quirky features such as an attractive chimney
breast or an intricate cornice.

STENCIL LIKE A PRO

❋ **Use the right equipment**
Stencilling brushes are round with short, stiff bristles. Use them in rapid up-and-down movements to dab paint onto your stencil. This helps prevent paint from seeping under the edges. A sponge or small roller will also do the trick.

❋ **Work from the outside in**
Start on the edges of the stencil, working into the centre, rather than from the centre outwards. Again, this helps prevent paint from leaking under the edges as you are less likely to accidentally bump the brush against an outline.

❋ **Try not to go overboard**
Don't overload your brush with paint as this can also cause it to leak under the edges of the stencil. Load the brush lightly, so that the ends of the bristles are covered evenly; wipe off any excess on a piece of paper or cloth first, before applying it to the stencil.

❋ **Repeat performance**
You'll get far better results by applying two thin coats rather than one thick one. Wait for the first application to dry before applying the second. Patience is a virtue.

❋ **Stick with it**
Keep your stencil in place by taping it at the top and bottom. Use low-tack tape as it is easy to remove and shouldn't pull off paint from the wall surface.

❋ **Different colourways**
To use more than one colour in a stencil, use low-tack tape to mask off areas of the stencil you want to paint a different colour.

❋ **Do a trial run**
If you are using various stencils together, try out your design on a piece of paper first. It is much easier to find out that something is not working at this stage and then correct it than when you are painting the real thing.

❋ **Keep it clean**
If you're doing a repeat design, wash your stencil regularly in warm water to ensure that the edges remain paint-free. If there is some paint on an outline, you will be unable to achieve a crisp edge to your painted motif. As paper stencils don't lend themselves to washing, acetate stencils are better for repeat designs. With a paper or card stencil, wipe off excess paint then leave to dry before using it again.

❋ **Sensible storage**
A stencil must be kept completely flat to be reusable. To prevent it from buckling, place it between two pieces of card and store it between the pages of a large heavy book, such as an encyclopedia.

FAR LEFT Offering a radical departure from the restrained and often tight formations of the 1980s, today's more organic stencils unfold across walls and floors in an apparently random display of pattern and colour.
LEFT Continuing this stencil design across different media – from the wall, round a corner and onto the bedhead – is as clever as it is quirky.

mood lighting

As every romantic is aware, thoughtful illumination is vital for creating a seductive atmosphere. After all, who could possibly relax in a dingy, badly lit space, or feel flirty in the glare of a harsh neon strip? The alternative is to opt for artificial lighting that creates indirect pools of warmth in some areas, while leaving others shadowy. Specific task lights that create an intimate glow are an excellent way of achieving this, while the subtle illumination of uplighters is preferable to harsh overhead styles.

If aesthetics rather than ambience is your primary concern, you'll find a wealth of choices available. First up is the antique chandelier, a firm favourite, thanks to its graceful combination of wrought-iron curlicues and frosted drops of clear or brightly coloured glass. Chandeliers range in style from extremely ornate to relatively simple – and while larger models make a wonderful centrepiece, smaller, less obvious examples, in the form of wall and table lamps, are also effective.

Wrought-iron candelabras – with their fake candles nestled amongst intertwining flowers and leaves – are similarly appealing, while other romantic illuminations include floral fairylights, which can be trailed across mirrors, picture frames and mantelpieces. Table lamps sporting sweet floral shades also work well in romantic room sets – as do modern light installations such as Tord Boontje's Garland design, which comprises intertwining metal flowers and leaves that can be wrapped around a lightbulb.

For truly romantic illumination, candlelight is by far the best option. Providing a shadowy intimacy, its flickering glow is impossibly flattering – giving off an alluring ambience that cannot be re-created artificially. For best results, group a cluster of candles, varying their size and shape to add perspective. Votive styles will lend a spiritual feel, while candles with embedded petals compound the floral vibe.

PRETTY PANELS

Because the sensitive harnessing of natural light is a key feature of floral boudoirs, it makes sense to dress your windows with floaty drapes. Lengths of semi-transparent fabric that diffuse the light, such as muslin, voile, net or lace are ideal, and have the added advantage of stirring seductively in the breeze.

All you need to make floral drapes is:
* **voile or organza fabric**
* **silk flowers is varying sizes**
* **curtain rod**

* Cut the fabric to size, allowing extra at the top for inserting the rod and 2cm (¾in) at the bottom for a double hem, plus a 1cm (½in) hem allowance on both sides.
* Press under a 1cm (½in) hem allowance on both sides of the curtain and stitch.
* Fold under a 1cm (½in) hem at the bottom of the curtain. Turn under again, then press and stitch.
* Fold under and press the top raw edge, then fold again to make a channel for the rod, and stitch.
* Position the larger flowers on the panel and stitch them neatly in place. Repeat with the smaller flowers.

ABOVE Decorating a voile panel with a random pattern of silk flowers is a great way to enliven a basic window treatment.

OPPOSITE A pretty glass light adds an original decorative element.

rosy seats

Although floral patterns provide the perfect foil for a diverse range of furniture styles, antique pieces are the best option if you want your boudoir to resonate with romanticism. Not only do slipper chairs, chaises longues and ottomans add a sense of old-fashioned glamour, they also provide an excellent dumping ground for clothes and bags. Wicker furniture, preferably painted white, also works well, imbuing feminine bedrooms with a refined sense of rusticity. In addition, wicker pieces provide an excellent complement to floral upholstery, while the introduction of French furnishings is a great way to add a little ooh-la-la. Think wrought-iron daybeds, Louis XIV armchairs, armoires and gilt-framed mirrors propped against the wall.

ABOVE A chunky floral mattress and scattering of bold cushions soften the stark lines of this vintage daybed.
OPPOSITE Give antique chairs a new lease of life by reupholstering them in a modern fabric.

feminine fripperies

Although romantic details are a defining feature of floral boudoirs, it is important not to overdo it on the frou-frou front. A few carefully chosen mementos will have a far greater impact than a mass of meaningless knick-knacks, while accessories with an old-fashioned bent will evoke a sense of timeless femininity. Good ideas include furnishing your dressing table with a monogrammed vanity set, covering the backs of chairs with delicate lace cloths, or dotting the mantelpiece with sepia photographs in a selection of pretty antique frames.

If you're lucky enough to have high ceilings, use the tops of cupboards and armoires to show off floral hatboxes or a collection of vintage textiles. Alternatively, showcase ornaments in a glass-fronted cupboard or hang a floral tea dress on a padded hanger to create an art installation that is as fashionable as it is aesthetic. You could also tuck flowery postcards inside a picture frame or display scraps of your favourite antique chintz beneath a glass-topped table.

FRAGRANCING YOUR INTERIOR

Ensuring that your home smells as sweet as a summer garden is an integral part of modern decorating schemes. Indeed, contemporary practices such as lighting a perfumed candle or spritzing the bedlinen with lavender water have become as natural as squirting fragrance on your wrists, while matching your scent to your décor is one of the most attractive ways to complete a design scheme.

Because of their associations with love, floral fragrances work particularly well in interiors with a feminine slant. Aromatic flowers such as carnations, mimosa, frangipani and honeysuckle are guaranteed to create a heady ambience, while the aphrodisiac properties of rose, narcissus and neroli have long been exploited for their ability to seduce and beguile.

Burning an aromatherapy candle is one of the most effective ways of scenting your space, as the fragrance will linger for hours after the flame has been extinguished. Although there are many different types of candle on the market, it's worth shelling out on the more expensive varieties, which do not emit the ghastly synthetic scents of cheaper products. In addition, investing in a pricier candle guarantees more burning hours, as well as producing a stronger, more authentic, fragrance.

Alternative olfactory products include chi-chi home-fragrance sprays, which come beautifully bottled in elegant glass flacons. Indeed, the trend for scenting interiors has taken off to the extent that a number of top fragrance houses are now producing scents that can be sprayed on sheets, carpets, towels and upholstery, as well as your skin.

If you prefer sprays that are more naturally scented to those you can buy in the shops, why not create your own home fragrance? Fill a clean plant mister with 150ml (5fl oz) of warm water and add five drops of your favourite essential oil. Shake the mixture vigorously before spritzing into the air.

> **TIP:** Slip cotton bags filled with fragrant dried flowers inside loose covers to deliver a waft of scent as you sink into the chair's squashy depths.

OPPOSITE Keeping to a pale palette prevents this eclectic mix of details from appearing overly fussy. The fringed shawl introduces a softer element, which is echoed by the pleated lampshade and pretty nightdress displayed on a delicately patterned hanger.

ABOVE LEFT A floaty dress and a selection of floral bags and hats create a fashionable art installation along this panelled wall.

fresh florals

The best way to enhance a floral decorative scheme is through the inclusion of real-life flowers. Not only do freshly cut blooms add fragrance and colour to modern interiors, but they are also easily available, relatively cheap and gratifyingly simple to arrange.

While jolly chrysanthemums and splashy sunflowers are excellent ways to inject your home with a sense of vibrancy, the feminine look calls for a more subtle approach. Although 'old-fashioned' flowers such as wild roses, daisies, pansies and tulips tend to look better in solo displays, it is possible to mix and match blooms, so long as you ensure that they are of a similar hue. It's also advisable to make floral displays look as though they've been casually thrown together; as a general rule of thumb, haphazard arrangements look much more appealing than structured ones.

Flower shops are gradually realizing the value of simple blooms and it's now possible to buy seasonal branches of blossom, forsythia, rosehips and catkins, in addition to a variety of showier stems. These single blossoms are bought, or cut, in bud in order to prevent their delicate petals from becoming damaged when you arrange them. Buying botanicals in this way also means that you have the pleasure of watching the buds slowly unfurl.

The containers you use to put flowers in are almost as important as the blooms you choose to display. These range from cut-glass, china or ceramic vases to elegant single-stem styles. Steer clear of conventional vases in feminine interiors, however, as this introduces a formal note that is at odds with the ethereal feel. Instead, put wild roses in a cream mug, jasmine in an earthenware pot, and camellias in a floral teapot. Alternatively, fill a simple glass jar with a spray of honeysuckle or soften the lines of a sturdy zinc bucket with a bunch of eye-popping hollyhocks.

> **TIP:** Flower heads that are good for floating in bowls of water include lilies, orchids, roses and gardenias. Blooms and petals can be combined with floating candles shaped like flower heads.

LEFT Thread real rose heads onto twine for a decorative take on a traditional floral garland.
OPPOSITE Blowsy blooms breathe life into interiors.

'YOU MAY BREAK, YOU MAY SHATTER THE VASE, IF YOU WILL, BUT THE SCENT

OF THE ROSES WILL HANG ROUND IT STILL.' Thomas Moore, Irish musician and songwriter

framed florals

Decorating your walls with floral images is one of the easiest and most effective ways of introducing a botanical feel to your interiors. In addition, the wide range of choices enables you to create a variety of different looks – from sprawling montages that cover a single wall to delicate oils that can be dotted around the room.

If you want to evoke a sense of nostalgia, opt for watercolours from the mid- to late Victorian era. Featuring spontaneous still lifes, which appear to unfold across the canvas in an apparently random manner, antique water-colours are best displayed in plain gilt or elaborate gold-leaf frames. Alternatively, opt for a colourful selection of flower prints by the great eighteenth-century French painter Pierre-Joseph Redouté, or choose contemporary pastels, which will complement a delicate palette and compound the sense of fragility.

OPPOSITE This floral montage creates a soft focal point and complements the modern lines of contemporary furnishings.
ABOVE Single blooms displayed in a series of suspended vases offer a unique alternative to more traditional displays.

WALL MONTAGE

If you want to feature different floral images in a montage that gels rather than jars, you should:
※ Choose a variety of images but stick to a single flower type (mixing poppies with petunias is seldom a good idea).
※ Vary the size of the pictures.
※ Feature no more than three different colours.
※ Keep your montage free from the constraints of symmetry, in order to reflect the random appearance of botanicals.
※ Overlap pictures to give a spontaneous feel.
※ Juxtapose close-up shots with some full-size images.
※ Finally, don't forget trial and error, which will always unearth a successful solution.

DRIED FLOWERS

Drying and preserving flowers is an excellent way of providing your home with natural decoration. It's also a fundamentally simple process, which involves picking your chosen blooms, stripping them of their leaves and hanging them upside down to dry.
※ Flowers and other plant materials for drying should be picked close to their prime.
※ Always collect more material than needed, to allow for damage.
※ Use only the most perfect forms. Poor shapes dry as poor shapes.
※ Use only flowers that are free of disease caused by insects, as this becomes more obvious after drying.

※ Pick flowers when they are free of dew or rain. Place stems promptly in a container of water to prevent them from wilting while you're gathering other specimens.
※ Flowers continue to open as they dry, so make sure florals are not fully open when picked.
※ Tie flowers securely in bunches and hang upside down in a warm, dry location for two weeks.
※ Use rubber bands to dry flowers, as stems shrink during drying.
※ It is sometimes difficult to develop graceful lines when making dried flower arrangements. Therefore, look for branches and stems with sweeping curves that will add a distinctive feel. Curves can also be made by shaping the branches or stems into the desired positions while they dry.

SILK FLOWERS

Although real flowers breathe life and vitality into interiors, it's not always possible to furnish your home with a display of brilliant blooms. Luckily, silk flowers offer a viable alternative, thanks to their amazing ability to mimic the soft folds of genuine blooms. Indeed, faux florals are so realistic, it's often hard to distinguish between the real and the not-so-real (you can even have the petals sprayed with scent for extra authenticity). Better still, silk flowers are available in literally hundreds of different varieties.

OPPOSITE Pink walls create
an ultra-feminine boudoir.
LEFT Mix and match fabrics
for an eclectic feel.

bedrooms

Decorating with florals presents the perfect
opportunity to create ultra-feminine flights of
fancy. This is often most apparent in bedrooms,
where the desire to create a dreamily romantic
space can be hard to resist. And why should you
sacrifice your minimalist principles in order to
create a sigh-inducing sanctuary? Instead, choose
florals that convey a subtle sense of femininity,
and always remember: less is more.

Whatever your tastes, the bedroom should
convey a sense of ease and intimacy. After all,
this is the most personal space in the home,
a peaceful retreat where you can reboot mind,
body and soul. Therefore, the furniture and
furnishings you select for it should be cosily

indulgent – with the main emphasis on sensuous
curves, calming colours and pretty prints.

It goes without saying that your bed is a key
factor in the creation of a blissed-out boudoir:
not only does a good night's sleep help to restore
the spirits, but creating a comfortable nest is
also paramount when you consider that we
spend one third of our lives curled up under the
duvet. As a result, purchasing a quality mattress
is instrumental in achieving the best downtime
possible. Size is also important: beds should be
large enough – and luxurious enough – to spend
the weekend in, with romantic styles ranging
from curvy sleigh beds to magnificent four-
posters and antique French *lits*.

lush linens

Beds provide the perfect arena for showcasing floral fabrics, allowing for the creation of numerous different styles. If you want to keep your look low-key, for example, simply combine pale cotton or silk sheets with floral pillowcases and leave it at that; alternatively, mix and match darling buds with larger blooms, and top with a satin comforter. For a sweetly feminine look, twin bitsy sprigs with candy stripes, match floral curtains with scatter cushions, or plump vintage quilts on top of lace sheets.

One of the best ways to introduce texture and warmth is to layer the bed with antique fabrics – vintage eiderdowns combined with age-softened linen sheets are a great way to add a sense of timeless warmth, while a dotted floral duvet teamed with an old-fashioned car rug and a scattering of antique lace cushions gives a romantic feel.

To compound the loved-up look, drape lengths of muslin, voile or net from a ceiling corona so that the fabric falls over the bed in dreamy folds. Alternatively, hang floaty net drapes from a tiara-shaped frame set against the wall behind your bed.

OPPOSITE Canopied fabric introduces a sense of romance. LEFT Mix florals with polka dots for a playful effect.

SCENTS OF SEDUCTION

If you want to enhance the sensual appeal of romantic-style boudoirs, opt for scents with floral notes:

❋ **Rose**

Universally recognized as the quintessential symbol of love, roses have a seductive fragrance and have been used as an aphrodisiac for thousands of years: Cleopatra filled her bedroom with rose petals to lure her lover Mark Antony, while the Romans scattered them on the bridal bed to reduce first-night nerves. The pungent aroma of crushed rose petals is also believed to aid conception, as well as lift the spirits. For best results, vaporize the essential oil, or light a rose-scented candle.

❋ **Jasmine**

Like rose, jasmine, with its sweet, slightly narcotic perfume, is very costly, primarily because large amounts of flowers are required to produce even a small amount of oil. Best used in small doses, jasmine promotes relaxation, counters anxiety and depression, and also affects hormone production. Introduce it to your boudoir in the form of scented candles and incense sticks.

❋ **Ylang ylang**

The sweet perfume of ylang ylang, which means 'flower of flowers', is believed to be an aphrodisiac, thanks to its calming properties. Asian women use it to perfume their hair as a prelude to amorous encounters, while Westerners blend it with citrusy smells such as lemon and bergamot.

bathrooms

Viewed as a functional space rather than a recreational one, the bathroom is traditionally overlooked when it comes to decoration. Certainly, hard surfaces such as porcelain, chrome and enamel can be off-putting, but these elements can be easily balanced by softer, more feminine materials, helping to turn the most unconvivial of washrooms into havens of peace and tranquillity.

One way to soften bathroom fixtures and fittings is to include floral patterns that direct the eye away from sharp contours. A striking wallpaper depicting blowsy cabbage roses, for example, is guaranteed to soften hard edges, while a funky shower curtain will also create a visual diversion. The addition of floral fabrics is another way to introduce colour and texture to potentially sterile spaces. While flowery curtains work well in larger, country-style bathrooms, roller blinds are better suited to smaller spaces, and can be easily assembled from ready-to-make kits. You can use almost any cotton or linen, so long as it is treated with a stiffening spray.

If you're fortunate enough to have a large bathroom, use the space to create a softer, more relaxed environment. Capacious chairs with slipcovers in cosy towelling or hard-wearing denim are ideal for introducing a 'loungy' feel, while floral-print upholstery can dress up wicker sofas, stools and ottomans. Area rugs

also work well in larger spaces, helping to incorporate softness and warmth, while the new ranges of vinyl tiles – funky squares depicting photographs of roses, daisies and grass, for example – can brighten up smaller spaces.

Details make or break a bathroom. Install Victorian-style floral basins and baths (either reproductions or bought from reclamation yards) and add matching splashback tiles. Alternatively, add floral trims to towels or line linen baskets with spriggy fabrics. You could also put a flowered curtain around your washstand, hang floral-print laundry bags on the back of the door and introduce petal-shaped soap dishes.

TIP: A simple way to enjoy a scented bath is to wrap fragrant herbs and flowers inside a piece of muslin, tie it with string and hang it from the taps in running water. For a relaxing soak, try camomile or lavender.

OPPOSITE Spriggy wallpaper and an invitingly comfortable armchair soften minimalist lines.

RIGHT A pretty floral basin is the ultimate feminine fixture.

simple chic

Elegant and understated, simple chic celebrates the laid-back beauty of imperfection, and calls to mind grand European houses, where the aura of old money is witnessed by a proliferation of threadbare carpets, faded velvets and peeling paint. This lack of ostentation is also popular on the east coast of America, where old-fashioned beach houses sport a similarly timeworn aesthetic. Indeed, the faded grandeur of simple chic can be easily incorporated into a variety of different styles, as long as various ground rules are adhered to. Furniture should either be handed down through the generations or sourced from flea markets, while typical floral motifs include blowsy blooms and bitsy buds. The simple chic palette is also integral to the look, featuring sea and sky colours, together with lashings of white paint.

LEFT Floral fabrics depicting teensy buds or a single overblown bloom create a suitably relaxed feel.
OPPOSITE Floral wallpaper, mismatched furnishings and untreated wooden floorboards are the staples of simple chic style, while the delicate candelabra and ornate mirror add an appealing sense of antiquity.

delightfully dilapidated

To create a home that's delightfully dilapidated, it's essential that your furniture and furnishings are imbued with a sense of soul: simple chic is not a look you can buy off the shelf, but rather an eclectic furnishing style that should evolve naturally over a number of years.

This relaxed style works best in rooms that are light, bright and clutter-free. Start by painting the walls a space-enhancing shade such as duck-egg blue, wild rose or mint green, and follow by ensuring that your flooring is both neutral and natural – stripped boards, pale carpeting and coir matting are all ideal.

Another way to compound the sense of informal ease is to dress windows with ultra-simple curtains or blinds in a neatly sprigged pattern – a space-enhancing trick that has the added benefit of looking effortlessly stylish. If your rooms are well proportioned and have large windows, create a sumptuous effect by draping the tops of windows with generous swathes of fabric, so that they fall to the floor in a luxuriant puddle. Light fixtures are similarly informal, and range from grand chandeliers (don't worry if you're missing a few crystal drops) to slightly battered metal wall sconces in stylized floral designs.

Furniture in the simple chic interior has two defining features – it is both elegantly scruffy and singularly comfy. Distressed wooden tables and paint-chipped daybeds sit alongside squashy sofas and oversized armchairs, while soft furnishings are often shrouded with divinely rumpled slipcovers – another simple chic staple – which help to disguise a multitude of sins, from ugly lines to garish upholstery.

Although accessories play an important part in making the simple chic home feel warm and inviting, they rarely take centre stage. Instead, decorative additions look as though they've been casually thrown together rather than carefully arranged. It's also important that decorative details have a timeworn feel. Scour second-hand shops for accessories that are elegantly distressed. These could include vintage vases, old-fashioned clocks, paint-chipped candleholders and antique glassware. Fresh flower arrangements also have their part to play, with cottage-garden blooms such as daisies, pansies, and primulas taking precedence over fussy floral bouquets. Indeed, the ephemeral beauty of a simple bunch of roses cannot be overestimated, especially when the arrangement has reached that pretty petal-dropping stage.

OPPOSITE Matchboard panelling and a delicate pastel palette create a charming beach-house feel.

BELOW An eclectic display of ornaments grouped in front of a mirror completes the laid-back ambience.

make do and mend

One of the joys of trekking round antique fairs is spotting the potential of simple chic furnishings, and working out what can be revamped and what can't. Badly broken wicker and severely mottled mirrors fall into the latter category, while salvage items such as dining chairs are worth investing in, as introducing matching pieces is rarely a priority in the simple chic home. That said, it's advisable to look for similarity in height and design, and to make sure that chairs are sturdy enough to take your weight. Drop-in seat bases are another feature to keep an eye out for, as detachable seats are much easier to re-cover than ones you cannot remove. If you want to unify a selection of mismatched chairs, why not use the same floral print on each seat cover? Alternatively, opt for different botanical patterns to give your chairs a sense of individuality. For a truly floral feel, make tie-on chair backs that match your seat covers – a technique that works equally well on ladder-back chairs with woven-rush seats.

It's not difficult to breathe new life into items that have been sourced from antique outlets; all you need is a bit of imagination and a degree of decorative skill. For example, you can jazz up dilapidated dressers by adding floral-shaped drawer knobs in jewel-bright hues, or line the interior of a battered old trunk with a floral fabric, using a staple gun, drawing pins or fabric glue to secure it. As is so often the case, a lick of paint is a great way to disguise imperfections on wicker and wrought-iron furniture, while damage on the flat surfaces of small side tables or chests of drawers can be hidden by a piece of floral fabric held in place by a slab of glass.

If you fall in love with a second-hand armchair that has a couple of worn patches, cover the damage with an attractive throw rather than going to the expense of getting the entire chair reupholstered. Alternatively, use a treasured piece of your favourite floral fabric to re-cover worn patches; this technique works particularly well if the existing upholstery is also of a botanical nature, while mixing and matching flowery designs with striped and checked ones is equally effective. Not only is this a considerably cheaper option, but it also introduces an additional layer of texture and colour to your home, enabling your seating to become a decorative feature in its own right.

LEFT Floral cushions liven up simple furnishings.
OPPOSITE Salvage items such as paint-chipped furniture complement old-fashioned wallpaper designs.

pretty prints

Faded floral fabrics are an integral part of the simple chic interior, and provide the perfect complement to white-painted furniture, neutral floors and pastel walls. Ranging from blowsy roses to bitsy buds, and set against soothing backgrounds of sea green, silver grey and old-rose pink, they should be as softly appealing as a much-loved pair of old jeans.

Because they're so subtle, faded florals can be used on a wide variety of furnishings without appearing too overpowering. Better still, thanks to the vogue for prints that have been purposefully drained of colour, there are numerous designs to choose from. Whether you opt for a pattern from one of the new ranges of deliberately faded florals, or a vintage piece that's been genuinely sun-bleached, it's advisable to take a few swatches home before making a commitment. This way, you can judge whether the colour looks different in the light of your home, as well as noting how well it goes with other patterns and designs, including checks and stripes.

Fabric is one of the most striking ways to create ambience in a room, so you need to decide on the mood you want to create, and then experiment with fabric swatches, colours and patterns to see what works best. For a girlie look, team faded florals with mirrored furniture and botanical prints, or combine with tongue-and-groove panelling to create a beach-house vibe. If you want a fresh, pretty feel, mix faded florals with cut flowers and pastel-painted furniture (for best results, use eggshell paint, which has just enough sheen to be practical and washable, but avoids the over-bright glare of gloss).

OPPOSITE A floral tablecloth is timelessly appealing.

ABOVE Tiny buds are the *leitmotif* of simple chic style.

'ROSES ARE THE BEST PERFUME. THEY DON'T TAKE OVER A ROOM, THEY LAYER IT WITH SCENT.' Carolyn Quartermaine, interior designer

living rooms

The living room is the main room in the house and for this reason it is likely to be a hub of social activity – a place where family and friends gather together to exchange news, gossip and ideas. It is also a room for relaxing, where you can listen to music, talk on the phone or simply cogitate on your life. As a result, comfort and flexibility are key – helping to produce a chill-out zone that is as stylish as it is versatile.

The best way to create a relaxed lounging area is to eschew the formality of three-piece suites in favour of more casual arrangements. An eclectic combination of individual seating in different shapes and sizes – from tub chairs to squashy sofas and elegant chaises longues – is much more welcoming than the coordinated suites of less imaginative interiors. In addition, they can be easily reconfigured to suit a range of different social occasions.

The simple chic living room is calm and balanced – a place where the flow of energy is unfettered by overkill on the furnishings front. Low seating and tables compound the 'loungy' vibe, as do nineteenth-century metal daybeds, which look great with striped ticking mattresses and floral cushions. Leather furnishings also have a part to play in laid-back living rooms, thanks to their classic appearance and attractive durability, while wicker, available in a variety of weaves, promotes a similarly relaxed feel and works well in a wide variety of surroundings.

> **TIP:** Try flipping over a woven floral fabric. The underside can produce a wonderfully muted effect, perfect for that shabby look.

RIGHT Streamlined seating, lashings of white paint and wide floorboards all contribute to the sense of serenity in this fabulously spacious living area.

cool cover-ups

The epitome of simple chic style, slipcovered furniture is fashionable, functional and fuss-free. Traditionally used to protect chairs from wear and tear – as well as preventing upholstery from fading in the sun – cotton covers instantly transform the look of a room, introducing the sort of casual elegance that typifies simple chic style. In addition, slipcovers are an excellent way of hiding a multitude of sins, helping to disguise garish patterns and extend the life of threadbare sofas at relatively little expense. They can also be used to alter the appearance of furniture so that it fits a decorative agenda: for example, a cotton shift changes the proportions of a wicker sofa, helping it to look more substantial, while a boxy club chair can be transformed into an elegantly feminine seat through the addition of a slipcover with a pleated skirt.

Fabric-wise, it's advisable to choose a closely woven medium-weight material that's capable of withstanding a lot of hard wear. In almost every instance, cotton is the best choice as it is durable and easy to wash. Linen has an appealing texture, but pure linen wrinkles easily, so opt for a linen–cotton blend instead. The other advantage of natural fibres such as linen and cotton is that they cling to upholstery much more effectively than synthetic fabrics, as well as holding their shape better. For an elegantly draped effect, choose lightweight velvets, moires, muslins and poplin.

The fact that slipcovers can be taken off and washed adds to their appeal as repeated exposure to soap and water makes them look – and feel – increasingly tactile. Denim responds particularly well, as do chenilles and chintzes, which gradually lose their stiffness after washing, becoming softer and less shiny. It should also be noted that before any natural fabric is sewn up, it should be pre-shrunk, otherwise you may discover that your covers are too snug after their first laundering.

Whether you choose to cover your furniture in patterned or plain slipcovers is, of course, dependent on personal taste. Pale cotton covers sporting a splashy floral print will certainly add a dash of individuality, while opting for plain covers gives you the perfect excuse to include a barrage of blooming cushions; it's also possible to balance out a profusion of florals with one or two chairs covered in a plain colour pulled from the print. If you decide to use neutral fabrics, you can add interest through texture – quilted cotton, damask and linen all provide tactile variety, for example. Covering furniture in a pale colour also means that you need to make sure your existing upholstery is paler than your slipcover, or it will show through.

Although this look promotes simple furnishings, it is possible to incorporate a few flourishes without compromising the plain Jane premise. Variations on slipcovers include skirts with boxed or kick pleats, ruffles and flanges.

OPPOSITE Furniture slipcovered in neutral linen imbues chill-out zones with a homely feel.
ABOVE A floral armchair looks best in a plain room.

eating areas

The simple chic dining experience is an informal affair in which enjoyment is prized over etiquette. Tables tend to be large and scuffed as opposed to neat and gleaming, and seating is comfortable, although not necessarily uniform – Lloyd Loom wicker chairs can be teamed alongside wrought-iron garden seats, while small folding stools complement long wooden benches that have been dressed up with floral pads, cushions and throws.

While the timeworn patina of beautifully shabby tables deserves to be shown off, antique cloths also have a role to play. Darned and patched white linen is the smart option, while cotton styles trimmed with delicate lace provide

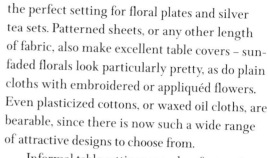

the perfect setting for floral plates and silver tea sets. Patterned sheets, or any other length of fabric, also make excellent table covers – sun-faded florals look particularly pretty, as do plain cloths with embroidered or appliquéd flowers. Even plasticized cottons, or waxed oil cloths, are bearable, since there is now such a wide range of attractive designs to choose from.

Informal table settings are a key feature in the dining arena, offering myriad decorating choices. To create textural contrast, mix a hotchpotch of china, glass and silver on a rough tabletop, or combine dainty floral teaware with hessian tablemats and chunky candles. For an ultra-feminine look, scatter petals freshly gathered from the garden over an antique tablecloth and add a selection of smooth white porcelain. Alternatively, place milky white china on a crisp, lace-trimmed tablecloth to create an old-fashioned feel.

China exerts the greatest impact on table settings – allowing you to create your own personal style from a wide array of different styles. Ideas include mixing the same floral pattern but in different colourways, or mixing and matching completely different patterns for a wildly whimsical effect. Another idea is to collect different pieces in a similar colour – dusty rose, for example – so that you end up with an eclectic set of plates, bowls and cups, all in the same faded pink.

> TIP: When buying china, look for pieces with elegant flowing lines: a good shape enhances all designs, regardless of colour or pattern.

LEFT An iron garden table is softened by a floral cloth and mismatched china.

OPPOSITE White paint unifies the utilitarian table and chairs, while the striped ceramics complement the white plates, glass tumblers and flowery cloth.

exotic florals

Although kitting out your home with exotic furnishings is hardly a new concept (Westerners have been importing silver, porcelain and lacquerware from the East since Roman times), it is an undeniably rewarding one, providing ample opportunity to create interiors that are as dramatic as they are distinctive.

Whether you favour the sleek modernity of **ASIAN GLAMOUR** or the itinerant appeal of **GLOBAL CHIC**, an exotic décor imbues rooms with a sense of immediacy, offering a vibrant alternative to the toning taupes and clean contours of modern minimalism. Vivid patterns and jewel-bright colours add a life-affirming feel while touchy-feely fabrics introduce textural interest. To complete the gadabout effect, introduce a selection of authentic global accessories.

Not surprisingly, florals fit the exotic profile perfectly – with cultural motifs ranging from stylized Indian roses to Chinese lotus blossoms and Caribbean hibiscus. Best suited to **BEDROOMS** and **DENS**, exotic florals can also brighten transitional areas such as hallways and stairs.

LEFT Japanese kimonos make beautiful wallhangings and soften the linear décor of this bedroom.
OPPOSITE A Shoji panel, Japanese tea set and some magnolia branches give this modern interior an Eastern feel.

fusing east and west

A far cry from Victorian times, when the practice of furnishing your home in 'exotic' style basically meant overkill on the chinoiserie front, today's interpretation places its emphasis on fusing different design elements from around the world. Particularly appealing to cool itinerant types who favour impromptu interiors over planned ones, furnishing your home with a vibrant cultural mix allows for liberated design schemes that juxtapose east with west and north with south to evoke feelings of warmth and spontaneity.

One of the main advantages of decorating with modern exotica is the relative ease with which the look can be pulled off. Requiring significantly less time and effort than numerous other design styles, its pick-and-mix approach allows for a relaxed, thrown-together look that can be as rambunctious or as restrained as you like. For example, a Javanese daybed scattered with kilim cushions will lend a genuinely ethnic ambience, while a fringed shawl draped over a chair or side table is the perfect way to give a semi-ethnic feel without compromising the Western aesthetic.

Opting for a global palette will also infuse interiors with a faraway feel. Mix fuchsia and scarlet with threads of gold for a sense of modern exotica, or combine dark earthy hues for a spicy oriental feel. Alternatively, team purples, reds and browns with modern furnishings for a hippie vibe, or fuse eye-popping Caribbean shades in magenta, ultramarine and yellow to conjure a sense of island life.

Like colour, fabric can instantly change the mood of a room, introducing warmth, pattern and texture. A key feature in the creation of exotic interiors, it is available in a wide range of global styles, including brilliant lengths of sari silk, Indonesian batiks, Japanese kimonos and Chinese chintz. Unsurprisingly, florals are a central motif in exotic interiors, imbuing modern room schemes with an organic energy that compounds the vibrant feel.

> **TIP:** Add potted orchids or sprays of blossom to enhance an oriental theme. Cut orchids will last for up to two weeks, as long as you remember to keep snipping the stems.

'I' THE EAST, MY PLEASURE LIES.' William Shakespeare

asian glamour

Although delicate vases and glossy lacquerware have been imported from the East since Roman times, it was not until the sixteenth century that trading links between Europe and Asia saw an influx of brightly coloured textiles. From China came sheeny silks embroidered with lustrous metallic threads, while India exported pretty, block-printed cottons that could be washed without losing their vibrancy.

Furnishing your home with orientalia is still popular to this day, although the modern interpretation is sharper and more streamlined than the intricate styles of yesteryear. Particularly popular with fans of colour and pattern, Asian style incorporates lustrous silks, flamboyant florals and ambient lighting.

LEFT The stylized blooms commonly depicted on Eastern fabrics are a quintessential feature of exotic interiors, adding a delicately graphic feel rather than a naturalistic one.
OPPOSITE A mix of floral prints gives this room a bohemian aura, while the classical statue provides a quirky contrast.

OPPOSITE A combination of black, white and red introduces a sense of exotica.
LEFT Prop a Chinese panel depicting cherry blossom on a dark wood mantel for a contemporary Eastern look.

oriental colours

While the Chinese view red as the colour of happiness, Westerners have always been wary of its aggressive connotations, fearing that an overkill of scarlet on the home front will stir up feelings of anger and resentment. Certainly, red has received its fair share of bad press over the years with design gurus warning that red bedrooms are likely to cause nightmares, while scarlet sitting rooms will almost certainly guarantee rows with your partner.

Whatever your feelings on the subject, it is an undeniable fact that scarlet interiors are not for the faint-hearted. That said, there are numerous shades of this fabulously rich hue – from cherry to cinnabar and burnt umber to brick – that will guarantee a vibrant colour injection without appearing dramatically over

the top. In addition, the seductive properties of fiery shades help to create a womb-like feel, imbuing your interior with a sense of cosiness and warmth.

Another way to incorporate red into your interior is by teaming it with similarly striking shades. The dynamic pairing of red and black has prevailed in Eastern design schemes for hundreds of years, while red and gold offers a slick sense of exoticism that cannot be rivalled. It's also possible to introduce various exotic hues through a handful of carefully chosen accessories. For example, the addition of an emerald wallhanging will pump up the pace in an instant, while a black lacquer stool or scarlet lampshade will give modern interiors a glamorous Asian feel.

low lighting

An integral feature of Asian décor, ambient lighting creates a seductive aura that helps to compound the laid-back, 'loungy' vibe. For best results, eschew the stark illuminations of modern track lighting in favour of a variety of light sources, which will create a series of glowing focal points around the room. It's also advisable to replace halogen spotlights, which tend to be too harsh for exotic design schemes, with softer, pendant styles that will emit a more subtle glow.

As a general rule of thumb, traditional lighting styles work best in exotic interiors, introducing a calming complement to the bright colours and vivid patterns of oriental décor. That said, a contemporary–modern mix is also effective, helping to compound the eclectic feel. A quirky or unusual light fitting adds an element of surprise, for example, and helps to provide a stylish contrast to more pedestrian styles.

For the most soothing illuminations, choose hanging lanterns, pendants or simple floor and table lamps. Not only do fixtures such as these cast intriguing pools of light and shadow, but they can also be individually controlled, allowing you to match your mood to your lighting. To enrich a vibrant decorative scheme, opt for wall lights, which create intense pools of localized colour. It's also possible to compound the atmospheric feel by using low-wattage bulbs, which will make saturated shades seem deeper and more luminous.

Coloured lighting is another option in exotic interiors, evoking a seductive feel that is an integral feature in Asian interiors. On a practical level, coloured lighting is also an extremely effective way of brightening up dingy corners, hallways and passages. Choose traditional Chinese paper lanterns, patterned with bright florals in shades of pink, yellow, red and green, or suspend a string of multi-coloured fairylights along a mantelpiece to create a playful party feel.

As is the case with a variety of decorative schemes, candlelight provides the most ambient of all illuminations – its flickering shadows evoking a sense of mystery and depth. For best results, cluster groups of candles together to create a feeling of spiritual intimacy, or place them in coloured-glass lanterns, so that they glow like a cache of exotic jewels.

TIP: Compound the seductive ambience of a moodily lit interior by burning candles fragranced with Eastern-inspired scents such as jasmine, orange blossom, frangipani, honeysuckle and lily-of-the-valley.

ABOVE LEFT A string of fairylights threaded through the bars of a wrought-iron bedhead give this glamorous boudoir a seductively ambient glow.

OPPOSITE Delicate floral motifs, combined with a spot of calligraphy, make for a pretty light fitting.

'THE KEY TO ORIENTAL STYLE IS TO CREATE A SIMPLE

BACKGROUND AND THEN ADD CONTRAST.' Kelly Hoppen, interior designer

flowers of India

Often cited as one of the most original and creative sources of patterned textiles in the world, the Indian subcontinent has been exporting fabrics to Europe and the United States for hundreds of years. Placing an emphasis on exuberant, brightly coloured designs, India's love affair with botanical patterns is an integral part of domestic life – with an exquisite profusion of floral decoration adorning textiles, floor tiles, rugs, stonework, furniture and architecture. To re-create a similar sense of abundance in your own home, choose fabrics and furnishings emblazoned with traditional Indian motifs such as tulips, lotus blossoms and flowers from the Tree of Life.

OPPOSITE Draped Indian shawls give the furniture in this elegant drawing room a wonderfully bohemian feel.
ABOVE Chintz has remained a popular furnishing fabric in Europe and America over the past 300 years.

CHINTZ

An enduringly popular fabric in British and American interiors, chintz was introduced to the West during the seventeenth century. Imported from the East Indies, its floral imagery and brilliant hues provided a sense of otherworldliness that was hugely appealing, while its shiny, dust-repellent finish made it a popular choice for curtains and upholstery.

Not surprisingly, English and French textile manufacturers began to develop their own versions of the fabric. Although the new-look chintz continued to feature natural motifs, the original loosely depicted patterns of flamboyant florals and exotic birds evolved to include tighter formations of cottage-garden blooms such as roses, daisies, sweet peas, tulips and carnations.

Today, there are chintz prints for every taste and décor, ranging from full-blown lilies to diminutive primroses. Additional patterns include romantic florals on delicately coloured backgrounds, and vibrant perennials set against one or two tones. The original chintz designs of the seventeenth and eighteenth centuries are still a ubiquitous feature in many modern interiors – their mellow sun-bleached appearance providing a warm lived-in feel. In fact, such is the demand for faded chintz designs that manufacturers are now artificially ageing fabrics to look as though they've been around for hundreds of years.

the silk route

Originally cultivated in China, silk became popular in Western design schemes during the nineteenth century, when it was snapped up by homeowners keen to inject their interiors with a touch of oriental glamour. Unsurprisingly, the wanton appeal of silk furnishings was an instant hit – introducing a sense of timeless opulence that compounds the extravagant approach of exotic design schemes. In addition, the enduring appeal of silk defies changing trends in home furnishings, enabling it to work as effectively in modern interiors as it does in traditional ones.

Available in numerous exotic shades – from mandarin orange to emperor purple – silk fabrics often sport floral motifs. These range from printed styles, as witnessed on Japanese kimono silks, to the more intricate embroidery of Chinese fabrics. For a truly authentic feel, choose traditional florals that have been used to represent the seasons for hundreds of years. These include a combination of bamboo, pine and plum blossoms for winter; iris or magnolia flowers for spring; peony or lotus blossoms for summer, and chrysanthemums for winter.

Embellished fabrics are another key feature in Asian interiors, providing a decorative element that adds character and originality. Better still, there are numerous applied fabrics to choose from, including intricate designs that combine appliqué with patchwork, together with more basic styles such as embroidered motifs on a plain background.

It is also possible to customize your own fabrics, thanks to the wide variety of decorative trimmings and accessories on offer. Ribbons, beads, buttons and bows are readily available from haberdasheries, while suppliers of Indian fabric sell a dazzling array of metallic threads, spangled braids and different-size sequins.

One of the best things about embellishing fabrics is the fact that almost anyone can do it. Simple additions, such as attaching velvet ribbon along the edge of a plain throw, can be achieved even by the most inexperienced of seamstresses, while tacking felt flowers onto a woollen cushion is similarly straightforward. To embellish your fabrics with ethnic sparkle, decorate them with beads, sequins and glass buttons; alternatively, trim lengths of cloth with tassels, satin cord or metallic ribbon to evoke a glittery harem feel.

> **TIP:** If silk is not to your taste, try one of its rich relations. Velvet introduces warmth and texture in a variety of shades, while devoré is similarly exotic, thanks to the chiffon floral patterns burnt into its deep pile. For a textural feel, opt for damask, which sports fruit and flower motifs in an intricate weave, or multi-coloured brocade patterned with delicate chinoiserie blooms.

ABOVE LEFT Chrysanthemums have been a favoured motif on Chinese silks for hundreds of years.
OPPOSITE Sari silk provides a romantic canopy for this magnificent gold and magenta bed.

chinese wallpaper

Chinese wallpaper has a long and venerable history in Western interiors, having graced the walls of grand European houses since the 1600s. Falling in and out of fashion during the intervening centuries, wallpaper is currently enjoying a revival – with styles ranging from traditional chinoiserie to modern exotica.

Reproduction papers of traditional Chinese designs are a particularly popular choice in contemporary homes. Featuring delicate repeat motifs of blossoms, birds and branches, they work especially well in grand hallways and formal drawing rooms, where their natural elegance enhances classical proportions. To create a seamless fusion between old and new, combine a traditional Chinese print with modern furnishings; alternatively, team with translucent colours, to help lift your look into the twenty-first century.

If the soft shades of jade green, sky blue and pale gold are a little insipid for your liking, why not try a splash of brilliant colour? Scorching pink peonies on an ebony background will create a seductive feel in dens and snugs, while graphic chrysanthemums on an emerald backdrop breathe life into transitional areas such as stairways and landings.

OPPOSITE Cherry blossom wallpaper and a fragile paper lamp prevent the dark wood table from appearing too imposing.
ABOVE Chinese wallpaper gives a hallway an oriental feel.

Creating a bedroom with soul is
simple, so long as you follow your
instincts rather than the dictates
of a glossy magazine. Indeed, it
is the juxtaposition of different
cultural elements that is the
cornerstone of global style.

✽ The presence of fabric adds
warmth and texture. Traditionally
used to insulate homes from the
cold, wallhangings have a decorative
rather than functional purpose in
contemporary interiors. A single
wall hung with a rich fabric can
make a sophisticated statement,
for example, while layers of
shimmering textiles help to build
a sense of mystery and intrigue.

✽ Rugs are the quintessential
floor covering in ethnic interiors,
introducing feelings of warmth and
domesticity. The rich colours and
intricate patterns of Persian kilims
add a layer of textural interest,
while hand-woven oriental designs
provide a decorative focal point.

✽ Enhance the appearance of
exotic fabrics by complementing
them with a range of similarly
themed ornamentation. The
delicate perfection of cherry
blossom is suited to bedrooms,
where the contrast of soft blooms
on wintry branches provides the
perfect touch in minimalist interiors.

✽ A selection of Japanese blossom
prints is the ideal accompaniment
to a kimono wallhanging, while a
Chinese floral vase will enhance
the intricate appeal of silk-
embroidered linen.

bedrooms

Traditionally soft and sybaritic, bedrooms are
the perfect place for displaying a variety of
exotic textiles. Used for seat and cushion covers,
as well as bedlinen and tablecloths, luxurious
materials such as velvet, brocade and damask
soften the strong lines of a modern décor, while
floral fabrics transform design schemes from
simple to sumptuous in an instant.

If you want to create a boudoir that resonates
with exoticism, silks from India, Cambodia or
China are a must, and they're available in
numerous luminous shades. Curtains in moody
violet or a chair upholstered in palest gold give
an extravagant feel, while silk sheets add an
inimitable sense of glamour. If you want to
incorporate an exotic feel but are wary of too
many bright colours, introduce accents of
exotica instead. A scattering of bright cushions
on a neutral sofa or a floral throw tossed over
the back of a chair will both do the trick.

One of the best ways to transform your
bedroom into a feel-good zone is to incorporate
a rich variety of seductive textiles. Soft and
enveloping, fabrics such as velvet, damask
and devoré are as attractive as they are sensual.
To complete the look, cover one wall with a
floral wallhanging or team velvet drapes with
a richly embroidered quilt.

A bold contrast of materials is another key
feature: a length of filmy netting draped over a
cane bedframe provides a pleasing mix between
floaty and functional, while a crewel-work
bedspread placed on top of satin-trimmed sheets
juxtaposes rough with smooth. It's also possible
to create contrast through the introduction of
pattern – a gallery of Audubon prints will enliven
a bare boudoir, while bold-scale chintz cushions
on a contemporary sofa will soften sleek lines.
For a more restrained effect, drape a side table
with a length of plain cloth and cover it with a
smaller piece of chintz. This suggests a sense of
organic abundance without going over the top.

OPPOSITE A beautiful screen
provides the perfect complement
to the blue-and-beige colour
scheme of this modern bedroom,
while ambient lighting helps to
compound the sense of serenity.

global chic

Thanks to the increase in travel opportunities and advances in communications systems, global style is fast becoming the decorative scheme *de jour* – with homeowners adapting a variety of exotic design elements to their interiors. Indeed, our heightened appreciation of different cultural heritages is such that it is now perfectly acceptable to juxtapose a Balinese table with an Islamic mirror or a French armoire with a Turkish kilim.

The belief that home décor should reflect personal style is a key feature of global style. Instead of following established guidelines, contemporary homeowners want their schemes to reflect who they are and what they believe in. By allowing your heart to rule your head, it's possible to create a global interior that incorporates different cultural elements within a modern framework.

LEFT Simple stylized florals in meandering designs add an itinerant feel, as do the neutral colours.

OPPOSITE A graphic screen is the focal point in this sitting room, while the carved desk and bamboo ladder add a sense of exotica.

floral artistry

Applying floral designs directly onto walls in the form of murals or painted decoration is an age-old practice that has been replaced by the fashion for framed pictures. However, the current emphasis on interior design schemes with soul – in addition to our preoccupation with all things natural – has resulted in a trend for botanical paint effects that have been customized to suit specific design schemes.

Wall-size depictions of flowers, leaves and branches are perennially popular because they offer an attractive aesthetic that's easy to replicate. Botanicals such as roses and daisies are relatively simple motifs to render onto walls, while oriental lotus flowers and chrysanthemums lend themselves particularly well to this medium, suffusing interiors with a sophisticated sense of exoticism. One of the simplest motifs is the cherry blossom. The national flower of Japan, this delicate bloom is revered for its fragility and transience (Japanese cherry blossoms open all at once, and the petals fall after about a week or ten days.) Unsurprisingly, it has inspired Eastern artists for generations, and looks just as attractive on Western walls as it does on oriental furnishings.

FREEHAND PAINTING

Wall paintings have a spontaneity that even the most beautiful stencilling cannot match. However, many people are understandably nervous about putting their artistic skills to work. To make the job easier, you need to be realistic in your choice of design – flat, two-dimensional treatments that rely on shape and colour rather than modelling and perspective for their effect are easiest to achieve. And remember, you don't have to paint anything strictly representative – it's shape, colour and form that are important, not botanical realism. As a result, even amateur artists can pull off a decorative paint job, so long as they work within their technical limitations, and stick to a few guidelines:

✽ Paint your floral decoration on a focal wall, but make sure that it's not too big, otherwise it will become abstracted or get lost.

✽ Restrict a painted design to one wall only. A scene that engulfs the entire room is likely to create an overwhelming and claustrophobic feel.

✽ There are no hard-and-fast rules about proportion. Instead, use your eye to determine the most pleasing result.

✽ Remember, botanical representations do not have to be accurate. One of the joys of painting freehand is the fact that a little stylization will almost certainly increase the arty effect.

OPPOSITE An oversized lotus flower makes a bold statement in the centre of a stripped wooden floor, introducing an unusual decorative element.
THIS PAGE A hand-painted branch of cherry blossom creates an appealing backdrop in this modern bathroom and softens the stark lines.

eastern florals

As a general rule of thumb, Eastern floral arrangements tend to focus on the beauty of one or two blooms rather than a variety of specimens, which are a frequent feature of Western displays. As a result, the exotic interior benefits from striking arrangements such as a single tiger lily in a clear vase or a collection of willow branches in a decorative Chinese pot. Alternatively, brighten up a dark corner with a life-affirming orchid or float a gardenia in a bowl of water and surround it with a selection of candles in different sizes.

It's also possible to change the feel of a room through the introduction of mood-inducing flowers. If you want to thwart negative energy, for instance, arrange a bunch of peace lilies in a transparent container and surround them with lots of space. To harness feelings of love and romance, display a single rose in a simple single-stem vase; alternatively, place bamboo shoots in an earthenware pot if you are in need of some good luck.

Exotic flowers lend themselves particularly well to solo displays, their vivid colouring and pure shapes serving to create exquisite pieces of living art. Offering the perfect option for those who are short on time or money, single-stem arrangements are quick and easy to effect; really, all you need to do is make sure that your flower is cut to the right height in order for it to be shown off to its best advantage.

It's also important to select your containers with care. Plain receptacles such as clear vases, test tubes, milk bottles and tall drinking glasses are all ideal, helping to compound the elegance of Eastern floral arrangements, without detracting from their singular beauty.

'EARTH RETURNS. KISSES FROM SKY. IN BLOSSOMS.' Haiku poet

LEFT Single stems in simple containers are a hallmark of oriental floral displays.

OPPOSITE A glass vase filled with exquisite blooms breathes life-affirming energy into this modern interior.

LEFT Tropical florals are depicted in stinging shades of pink, orange and blue. **OPPOSITE** Floral cushions, filmy netting and bleached wood create an exotic feel in this castaway bedroom.

tropical florals

The tropical look is a popular theme in home furnishings, drawing on influences from island paradises such as the West Indies, Bora Bora, Tahiti and Hawaii. Indeed, such is the appeal of these far-flung locales, it is no wonder that tropical style has become such a hit with contemporary homeowners.

Focusing on an intense profusion of pattern and colour, island décor is cool, vibrant and fairly easy to re-create. It's best suited to rooms that are awash with natural light – key features include lots of white and coloured paint, wicker furniture, floral cottons, bleached wood, lace curtains, patterned linoleum and antique maps.

Unsurprisingly, the introduction of bright colours is the fastest way to create an authentic tropical feel. Shades of vibrant turquoise, stinging yellow and emerald green are vividly reminiscent of island life, while the hues of exotic plant species such as bougainvillaea, hibiscus, poinsettias and philodendrons inspire floral shades of pink, orange, red and purple.

To create a genuine Caribbean feel, bright paintwork is a must. Window frames picked out in a vibrant hue will pump up the pace in an instant, while door panels can be similarly enhanced by a splash of brilliant paint. Another way to suggest a tropical feel is to remove an integral door and replace it with a bead curtain. Alternatively, use a translucent panel of floral fabric and attach it by ties to the door frame to create the sense of a breezy thoroughfare. To take the effect a step further, replace solid interior doors with hinged pairs of louvred panels painted in light pastel shades.

To complete the hot-country look, furnish with a selection of bright accessories. A coral pink radio, a thermos patterned with frangipani, or a garland of plastic flowers are all that's needed to evoke a playful sense of tropicana. Floral prints also work wonders, while distressed paint is another feature of island style. As a result, keep your eyes peeled for picture frames, chairs and tables in patchy shades of violet and pistachio.

dens

To create a living area with a global feel, it's essential to include a variety of far-flung furnishings. Items such as carved wooden tables, desks inlaid with mother-of-pearl and divans covered with floral throws all fit the bill, as do lacquered chests and Japanese futons. To evoke a colonial feel, include cane and wood pieces – these were first introduced to Europe by the East India Company in the seventeenth century.

As practical as they are pretty, daybeds offer the ideal seating option in ethnic dens. Set against a wall in order to maximize space, they provide an extra sleeping area for overnight guests, as well as presenting the perfect showcase for a variety of exotic fabrics. Cushions are another option, helping to dress up drab daybeds in an instant. To create back rests, simply pile the arms at either end with a selection of flowery pillows.

The classic chaise longue also works well in ethnic dens, its swooping back and low elevation suggesting a laid-back, 'loungy' vibe. To complete the look, furnish it with fabrics in contrasting florals, or up the glam factor by juxtaposing velvet upholstery with throws embellished with beads, sequins and tassels. Even modern sofas can be given an ethnic makeover. New upholstery in painterly florals will evoke a moody bohemian look, while layered fabrics – from mirrored Indian cloth to embroidered shawls and floral kilims – help to create a sense of depth and intrigue.

For a blinds-down, lights-out kind of look, choose ambient illuminations that will evoke an intimate feel. A fringed shawl tossed over a light shade will give your den a seductive aura, while Noguchi-style paper lanterns emit a soft glow that is equally evocative. For a Far Eastern flavour, opt for shades delicately crafted out of bamboo, or re-create the sense of balmy nights with a galaxy of twinkling tea lights.

TIP: If you plan to theme your room around a selection of flamboyant floral cushions, make sure that they are large enough to carry off bold motifs.

THIS PAGE A cane sofa covered with a brilliantly patterned fabric gives this breezy sitting area a happy Hawaiian feel.

funky florals

While quaint rose prints and darling sprigs will always be popular, what looks freshest today is their aesthetic opposite – graphic plants and stylized flowers that are as flash as they are funky. Indeed, nothing changes the look of a room as quickly as a brilliant splash of pattern and colour – but remember, a little goes a long way.

Best suited to sleek, modern interiors, funky florals are not for the faint-hearted. Whether you opt for **MODERN GRAPHIC** style or a look that resonates with **DESIGNER CHIC**, decorating with bold botanicals provides the perfect complement to stark minimalist spaces, injecting them with life and vibrancy.

Funky florals work best in minimalist spaces, where their ebullience is guaranteed to have maximum impact. Functional areas such as **KITCHENS** and **BATHROOMS** are ideal, while pared-back **LIVING ROOMS**, preferably with high ceilings and wooden floors, provide the perfect canvas for eye-catching prints on walls, floors and soft furnishings. To complete the look, add a selection of graphic accessories such as lampshades, ceramics, cushions and throws.

bold botanicals

Furnishing your home with funky florals need not be overwhelming, so long as you stick to a few basic guidelines. Firstly, start with a pattern, fabric or motif that you love, and then use it to make a singularly bold statement. A wallhanging depicting a graphic bloom has a truly modern edge, and can be used to make a striking focal point, for example. By the same token, restricting the use of a vibrant fabric to a smaller area, such as a cushion cover, is an effective way of kickstarting a neutral interior.

For a decisively modern look, contrast is key: clashing colours such as pink and scarlet will always be successful because no one colour predominates. It's also important to remember that while strong shades can appear over-powering, they are often easier to work with than subtler hues, which can be harder to define. That said, homeowners who cannot abide the idea of living with eye-popping shades of purple and orange can opt for bold botanicals

in earthier tones, which can be equally life-affirming and give a softer, more feminine feel.

Funky florals can be used in a wide variety of applications, including wallpaper, a medium that is currently enjoying a fabulously modern makeover. Ranging from bold botanicals that have been produced in the traditional way, to designs that have been created using the latest, digital techniques, the selection is as varied as it is vibrant. Indeed, modern technology has revolutionized wallpaper design to such a degree that it's now possible to buy floral motifs on a more exuberant scale than was previously thought possible.

Fabric-wise, funky florals are best treated simply. Rugs featuring stylized flower motifs create a warm counterpoint to polished wood or stone floors, while vigorously patterned upholstery breathes new life into soft furnishings. One of the advantages of covering furniture with funky fabrics is the surprise element: reupholstering the seats on antique dining chairs with a splashy floral adds a wonderfully modern-retro feel, while using a contemporary abstract on a fifties sofa provides an interesting juxtaposition between old and new.

Solo displays of simple cut flowers are a great way to complete a funky interior. Offering a complementary splash of colour, they should be used to enhance bold design schemes, rather than make a decorative statement of their own. Thus, a vase of gerberas softens the harsh lines of modernist kitchens, while a basic bunch of black-eyed Susans echoes the hues of a yellow and black wallhanging.

ABOVE Striking lampshades funk up this rustic-looking room.
OPPOSITE The bold colours and oversized motifs depicted on this ultra-modern print are used to create a design scheme that is as dramatic as it is daring.

'NOBODY SEES A FLOWER, REALLY; IT IS SO SMALL, WE HAVEN'T TIME, AND IT TAKES TIME – LIKE TO HAVE A FRIEND TAKES TIME.' Georgia O'Keefe, artist

modern graphic

The modern graphic look is both sleek and sophisticated. At the opposite end of the spectrum to country-cottage style, it appeals to homeowners who favour sprawling urban spaces over cosy cluttered ones.

The primary elements of modern graphic style include a monochrome palette, streamlined furnishings, and wallpapers and fabrics depicting stylized floral patterns. Digitalized images featuring oversized blooms are also integral to the look, while modern artworks in acid-bright hues provide an arresting focal point on stark white walls. Alternatively, you can use modern screens and funky bead curtains to introduce accents of pattern and colour.

LEFT Bold repeat motifs, a plain background and a minimal palette are the hallmark of funky floral designs.
OPPOSITE An ultra-modern fabric by British designer Jasper Conran give this classically shaped sofa an instant update.

OPPOSITE Digital designs can be used on furniture as well as walls.
LEFT Outsized photographic images offer a modern spin on traditional wallpaper.

digital florals

Digital technology has sparked the biggest wallpaper revolution since the first wallpaper printing machine was patented in 1839. As a result, canny computer users are now able to play around with size and scale, producing wallpapers that are radically different from the rambling patterns and repeat motifs of yesteryear.

Customizing images to suit the walls of your home is also becoming increasingly popular, and a growing number of businesses are producing designs to order. Capable of turning simple floral patterns into throbbing masses of abstract colour, digital technology also allows for the manipulation of photo-graphic images. This technique is particularly successful with botanical prints, which can be dramatically enlarged to reveal intricate details such as veining, mottling and bristling hairs.

It's also possible to transfer realistic floral images onto fabrics, thanks to recent advances in laser printing. Offering a vibrant sense of immediacy, a close-up of a brilliant flower head makes a striking motif on a plain blind, for example, while transferring photographic florals onto cushions brightens up a neutrally upholstered sofa in the same way that an abstract painting breathes life into a blank wall.

Hologram projections – the twenty-first century's answer to the photomural – are another way of introducing larger-than-life florals into your home. To change the look and mood of a room at the mere flick of a switch, all that's required is a projector and a selection of transparencies, such as flower-filled fields, alpine meadows or exotic blooms from far-flung countries.

blooming banners

If you like the concept of funky wallpaper but don't want to commit to all-over coverage, why not incorporate a decorative banner instead? Offering one of the most effective ways to introduce an arresting focal point, a single vertical strip takes on the prominence of a work of art, as well as creating an interesting sense of contrast between the pattern contained within the banner and the plain wall behind it.

Currently sporting motifs large enough to fill one drop of paper, contemporary designs include a graphic selection of oversized florals. Bold botanicals in acid hues are very popular, in addition to free-ranging designs that appear to climb the walls. For best results, choose screen-printed styles, which involve the production of small runs of exquisite handmade papers in which the patterns are large enough to render the repeats almost unnoticeable.

ABOVE Luminescent florals on a delicate Perspex banner contrast with the rough bricks on either side.
RIGHT The monochrome strip on the wall is repeated on the tabletop to create a sense of coherence in this dining room.

HANGING BANNERS

❋ Banners work best in minimalist rooms where their graphic appearance is guaranteed to have maximum impact.

❋ Use banners to add a new dimension to a room. For example, a collection of three vertical strips, hung at intervals, will break up a wide expanse of wall, while horizontal strips provide a counterbalance to high ceilings.

❋ If your space is on the small side, make sure that your banner is in proportion to other furnishings.

HANGING PICTURES

❋ Strong images need lots of space around them, so remove any unnecessary ornaments from the room, and keep furnishings and furniture to a minimum.

❋ Modern paintings look best hung on walls painted in a strong colour, which will bring them alive in a way that paler walls seldom do.

❋ When hanging a group, plan your arrangement by laying pictures out on the floor first, working from the middle picture outwards.

❋ If you're hanging a small group of pictures, keep the spacing tight.

❋ Don't dot pictures around a room, as they will look lost.

❋ When you're deciding where to hang a particular piece, sit or stand in the place where you spend most time to judge the effect.

❋ Theming pictures is an effective way of unifying a variety of different media, including prints, drawings and watercolours.

screen savers

A far cry from the fussy styles of the Victorian era, modern screens can still be decorative as well as functional. Indeed, contemporary room dividers are fast becoming an integral feature of twenty-first-century interiors, with styles ranging from Perspex panels to semi-translucent scrims.

Screens are best suited to larger rooms where they can be used to create a cosier, more approachable feel. If you want to make a feature of a room divider, opt for a traditional folding style featuring a riot of brilliant blooms on a startling white background. Alternatively, choose transparent room dividers, which will add a sense of structure to the interior without compromising on space and light.

TIP: Make your own funky room divider by covering a workaday screen with floral images cut out from magazines.

OPPOSITE A transparent screen etched with floral motifs introduces pattern and colour to this minimalist interior.
THIS PAGE Floaty scrims offer a fabulously funky alternative to more traditional room dividers.

blooming beads

Bead curtains are a great way of adding an element of fun to your interior. Available in numerous different designs – from strings of plastic flowers to bamboo panels painted with a floral design – bead curtains work best in open-plan living areas, providing a decorative divide between kitchens and living rooms, and bathrooms and dressing rooms.

If bead curtains are a tad unsophisticated for your liking, why not opt for Tord Boontje's ultra-modern take on traditional room dividers? Featuring a mix of flora and fauna, the talented Dutch designer's stunningly fragile-looking curtains are actually made from super-strong synthetic paper, which can be cut to the desired length with a pair of scissors.

ABOVE Tord Boontje's Screen creates a fabulous floaty feel.
OPPOSITE Bead curtains add a playful feel to funky interiors.

HOW TO MAKE A BEAD CURTAIN

Bead curtains are simple and easy to make. All you need is:

✳ **thick string**
✳ **floral patterned/shaped beads**
✳ **a dowel rod 10cm (4in) longer than the width of your doorway**
✳ **two hooks**

✳ Cut the string into pieces 20cm (8in) longer than you want the finished curtain to be, to allow room to tie knots in the string and to attach it to the rod.

✳ Tie a knot at one end of the string. This end will become the bottom of this curtain strand.

✳ Thread beads onto the string. The size of the beads determines how many you need. If you don't want your curtain to feature too many floral beads, introduce plainer styles, tying knots in the string after threading on each group of beads.

✳ When you have finished each length of bead curtain, tie a knot in the top end next to the last bead, ensuring that you have 15cm (6in) of string available for a loop at the top.

✳ To prepare your doorway for the curtain, attach a hook to the outside edge of the door frame on either side. Your dowel rod will settle into the hooks, making it stable yet easy to remove.

✳ Make a loop at the top of each finished strand and slide the dowel rod through. Place the rod into the hooks and slide each strand along it to create the right spacing.

✳ If you don't want your curtain pieces to slide around, tie them directly to the dowel rod rather than making a loop. This will attach the pieces more firmly to the rod and keep them in place.

OPPOSITE Floral drawer and cupboard fronts create a lively, lighthearted feel.

THIS PAGE A monochrome print stretching the width of the wall and an antique candleholder enliven this minimalist kitchen.

kitchens

In keeping with modern graphic style, the funky kitchen is sleek, chic and professional. Fitted units, smooth-sliding drawers and gleaming surfaces reflect the minimalist approach, while white goods (the washing machine, fridge and dishwasher) are artfully disguised behind a façade of streamlined panels.

The antithesis of their wholesome country cousins, funky-style kitchens feature top-of-the-range cookers and achingly hip appliances. This does not prevent the odd splash of brilliant pattern from breaking through, however. Indeed, bold botanicals are particularly well suited to industrial-style kitchens, their throbbing hues helping to soften the harsh lines of modern fixtures and fittings.

Not surprisingly, computer-generated images fit the look perfectly, with larger-than-life florals charging walls, floors and blinds with vibrant energy. Even ceramic tiles have been given a modern makeover, and include photo-realistic styles that provide a quirky contrast to smooth expanses of stainless steel.

Displaying floral china is another way of introducing pattern and colour to your cooking space. If you want to maintain the streamlined look, choose simple white plates with a minimal floral print on each. Alternatively, introduce chintz designs to provide a quirky element of surprise, or an eclectic selection of cups and saucers, which should be linked by colour, style or motif.

bathrooms

Originally viewed as a purely functional space, the bathroom has upped its profile over the past fifty years, evolving from the fashionable pastels of the sixties and seventies to the all-white vogue of the eighties – a look that has retained its popularity to this day.

The funky bathroom is coolly minimalist, combining streamlined fixtures and fittings with splashes of pattern and colour. For best results, team a white suite with built-in units to maximize space, as well as to create a blank canvas for decorative additions such as a bold botanical print or a screen decorated with floral motifs. If your bathroom is large enough, add a chair with a seat that has been upholstered in vivid fabric, or dress the window with a graphic floral blind. To create a more vibrant effect, paper or stencil the walls with a striking design – but remember to balance the look by keeping the rest of your furnishings plain.

Accessories can also be used to give wet rooms a funky twist. A graphic bathmat or shower curtain patterned with brilliant blooms is sure to kickstart neutral design schemes, while floral towels, a selection of modern ceramics or a brilliantly patterned laundry basket will all have a similarly striking impact.

BELOW Jazz up pared-back bathrooms with a blown-up floral photograph that will bring the outside in.
OPPOSITE A traditional screen painted with splashy blooms injects a jolt of energy into this white bathroom.

designer chic

Since the mid-1990s, when fashion designers started to diversify into home furnishings, the trend for hip homeware has snowballed. Kicking off with scented candles and the odd aromatherapy cushion, big-hitters such as Calvin Klein and Paul Smith are now stamping their sartorial signatures on bedlinen, cushions and ceramics. As a result, the fashion for designer homeware has filtered down onto the high street, with chains such as Nautica, French Connection and Monsoon producing photograph frames, towels and tablecloths. Not surprisingly, florals are big news in designer furnishings. As popular off the catwalk as on it, motifs range from exotic blooms to splashy silhouettes, and embroidered buds to retro sprigs.

LEFT Graphic floral motifs appeal to fashion designers who want their home furnishings to be as eye-catching as their clothes.
OPPOSITE Super-graphic upholstery – the ultimate in statement furnishing – is fast becoming a popular trend.

the fashionable look

The vast collection of Ralph Lauren, the king of floral fabrics, ranges from ponderous blooms to bitsy sprigs in navy, green and red. Designed to be mixed and matched with a variety of plaid, ticking and denim, Lauren's soft furnishings are the epitome of fashionable rusticity. Likewise, Tommy Hilfiger's Connecticut Farmhouse range, which combines bold florals with colourful checks and stripes, creates a similarly charming 'down-home' feel.

Fans of monochrome will love Donna Karan's Hibiscus bedlinen, which features graphic black florals on a white background. Offering the perfect solution for fashionistas who want their interiors to be as cutting-edge as their clothes, Karan's bedwear is at its most dramatic when combined with contemporary furniture and a stripped-wood floor. Alternatively, team it with dark drapes and a deep-pile carpet for softer, more seductive feel.

For ethnic glamour, try Kenzo Maison's home collection that takes its cue from African colours. Teaming floral-printed silks alongside a raft of textural fabrics in plum, ochre and cocoa, the Kenzo look suits smaller rooms such as studies and dens, where its moody hues and delicate detailing can be properly appreciated.

Renowned for his ability to combine modern tailoring with British romanticism, Jasper Conran produces home furnishings that are as sophisticated as his suits. Following the introduction of his ultra-sleek ceramics, the designer's new Sprig collection features stylized florals on gem-bright backgrounds. Available in fabric and wallpaper, Sprig works wonders in minimalist lounging areas, where its graphic impact breathes life into walls, sofas and chairs.

OPPOSITE Matthew Williamson's furniture is as funky as his frocks.
RIGHT Floral fabrics by Missoni (top) and Cacharel (below) are currently *de rigueur* in fashionable design schemes.

LEFT Lulu Guinness's rose rug brings this minimalist sitting room to life.
OPPOSITE A graphic floor covering by Diane von Furstenberg.

designer flooring

Thanks to the ongoing fashion for minimalism, floors have become an increasingly important feature in modern interiors, with stripped wooden boards consistently claiming the number-one spot. Indeed, such is the popularity of timber flooring that, up until recently, alternative styles have languished on the backbenches, with uninspiring styles ranging from prickly seagrass to ubiquitous oatmeal.

In response to this, contemporary designers are now producing a variety of funky floor coverings. Featuring bold botanical patterns, these new-look carpets include Cath Kidston's Rose Bouquet design, which depicts scarlet flower heads in full bloom on a bright blue background. For a more muted effect, choose her nostalgic Rosebud pattern, featuring quaint red buds on an 'antique white' background.

The best way to incorporate a boldly patterned carpet into your interior is to choose a design that provides the room with a colour scheme, then pick out individual shades and echo them with paints, fabrics and accessories. In smaller spaces it's best to use repeat motifs so the scale of the design can be matched by compact furniture and neat small-print fabrics.

If you are wary of using wall-to-wall pattern, stick to rugs, which contain the design within a defined area, rather than allowing it to take over the entire floor. For the funkiest styles around, visit The Rug Company for designs such as Diane von Furstenberg's realistic roses on a blood-red background, or Marni's Tibetan wool styles that feature a variety of naïve florals in pink, yellow and mauve. For a more graphic approach, choose Lulu Guinness's monochrome rose pattern, which looks fabulous on wooden floors, or Missoni's striped rugs, which can be mixed and matched with a variety of floral fabrics in similarly vibrant colours.

'FLOWERS OF ALL HUE, AND WITHOUT THORN, THE ROSE.' John Milton, poet

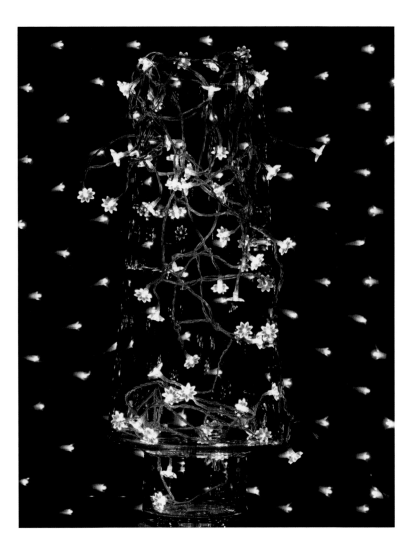

floral fairylights

Offering twinkly illuminations at the flick of
a switch, fairylights have a gaudy glamour that
is no longer confined to the Christmas tree.
Indeed, fairylights have fast become one of the
coolest accessories around, with hip homeowners using them to glam up a variety of
furnishings – from bedheads to bookcases.

Although basic white fairylights will
undoubtedly imbue your home with an
element of glitz, there's also a wide selection
of alternative designs to choose from. These
range from multi-coloured plastic flower shapes
to larger styles that have been fashioned into
replicas of vintage roses or striking hibiscus
heads. It's also possible to buy wall-sized nets
of fairylights, which offer a funky alternative
to traditional prints and paintings.

EIGHT WAYS TO DISPLAY YOUR FAIRYLIGHTS

✳ Give your interior extra sparkle
by draping a string of fairylights
across windows, doors, picture
frames and bookcases.

✳ Hang fairylights around a mirror
or above a working fireplace to
maximize the glittery effect.

✳ Trail a string of lights encased in
protective rubber tubing along the
floor to create a serpentine look.

✳ Twist fairylights into funky floral
shapes, and tack them onto the
wall using small cable clips. A naïve
flower head above a dressing table
makes a glittery focal point, while
clusters of all-white lights give the
impression of spring blossoms.

✳ Thread them through banisters
to liven up a dull staircase, or twine
them between slatted chair backs.

✳ Mix and match multi-coloured
lights with plain ones to create
a gaudy, fairground feel.

✳ Twist fairylights around plant
pots to glam up your greenery.

✳ Choose flashing designs to
create a seventies disco vibe.

> **TIP:** Fairylights should
> be treated with utmost
> care, as their delicate
> wiring frequently causes
> fuses to short-circuit.

OPPOSITE Fairylights draped across
a chair add a sense of romance.
ABOVE LEFT Tiny illuminations
create a funky disco feel.

living rooms

Effortlessly chic – as well as perennially fashionable – black-and-white design schemes are a great way to jazz up your interior. Whether you're seeking the full-on graphic effect or something a little less intimidating, the creation of the monochrome look allows for room sets that are as striking as they are seductive.

For best results, team off-white walls with soft black upholstery. To soften the effect, accessorize with floral cushions in contrasting shades of orange and red. Alternatively, you can combine white paintwork with a two-tone floral wallhanging and introduce accents of colour via lime green glassware or a turquoise throw. For a truly modernist feel, team a monochrome palette with materials such as suede and bouclé, which will add a sense of texture and warmth.

If you like the black-and-white look but don't want to go the whole hog, incorporate a single monochrome design feature and leave it at that. In order for this method to be truly successful, however, you must ensure that the other furnishings in the room balance out the look, and that any additional patterns collaborate with the overall effect.

Decorating with a select group of black and white accessories is another way of showing off your style nous. Items such as a chequered photo frame or a two-tone vase will introduce a gently graphic feel, while bunches of flowers are equally effective: use velvety black tulips to create a sense of sophistication, or a vase of dark purple pansies to compound a moody ambience.

TIP: To prevent coloured spines disrupting a sleek monochrome look, cover books with plain black or white jackets.

RIGHT Soft shades of black contrast with harsher ones to create an ultra-modern design scheme.

retro florals

In a world that is less than secure, there is something very comforting about retro designs. Lurid wallpapers that your grand-parents might have had bring a warm rush of recognition, while chunky ceramics patterned with sixties florals are similarly evocative, conjuring an era that was ablaze with energy and innovation.

Spanning the fifties, sixties and seventies, retro style is currently enjoying a renaissance, its bold patterns and vivid hues providing an appealing contrast to the sleek lines of contemporary living spaces. Indeed, the success of the modern retro look depends on the juxtaposition of old and new and patterned and plain.

Easily adapted to suit a variety of different architectural styles – from slick city apartments to rustic farmhouses – furnishing with retro pieces lends interiors a colourful sense of character and history. Ranging from the sleek linearity of **MID-CENTURY MODERN** to the ebullience of **FLOWER POWER**, the look is best suited to smaller rooms such as **WORK SPACES** and **SNUGS**, where its cosy familiarity can be exploited to the full.

LEFT Chunky ceramics are typical
of sixties style.
OPPOSITE A floral cushion and
shagpile rug warm up this
minimalist space.

flashback furnishings

Appealing to a new generation of collectors, the fashion for retro furnishings has been fuelled by the likes of interiors magazines such as *Elle Decoration* and *Wallpaper*, while Modernist props on popular TV shows like *Big Brother* and *Frasier* have compounded the trend.

In addition to this, people are redefining the way they live in the twenty-first century. New types of homes, such as minimalist loft-style apartments, are much better suited to the cool lines of Modernist furnishings, while bold floral patterns complement stripped wooden floors and neutral-coloured walls.

The fashion for collecting retro designs is also flourishing thanks to a wide variety of items now available from both the high and low ends of the market. Vintage pieces – ranging from inflatable chairs to fibre-optic lights – can be sourced from antique fairs and auctions, while smaller items, such as Whitefriars glass, Midwinter china and lava lamps can be found in flea markets and junk shops.

It is also possible to buy Modernist furniture from a select group of shops specializing in vintage design classics. The availability of retro furnishings has also increased: several furniture companies such as Herman Miller and Parker Knoll have reissued classic chairs, tables and sofas by various designers, including Verner Panton, Joe Colombo and Hans Wenger.

mid-century modern

Particularly attractive to home-owners who hanker after coolly minimalist interiors, the mid-century modern look is currently enjoying a resurgence, its fluid furnishings and neutral palette imbuing contemporary design schemes with a sense of authentic fifties style. Natural materials such as leather, wood and slate are also integral to the look, providing an earthy feel that adds texture and warmth, while graphically patterned fabrics introduce vibrant splashes of colour. The bold, stylized botanical motifs of fifties prints provide a striking contrast to the spartan lines of mid-century décor. Colour-wise, the focus is on organic shades of green, orange and brown, while occasional splashes of purple and red compound the retro feel.

LEFT Bold stylized botanicals in vivid hues are a quintessential feature of fifties design schemes.
OPPOSITE Wood-panelled walls and streamlined furnishings create a cool Scandinavian feel, while flashes of orange and green enliven the soothing cream environs.

the modern retro look

Best suited to light rooms with big picture windows or sliding glass doors, fifties interiors favour the less-is-more approach. As a result, it is essential that you clear your space to create a blank canvas for the addition of mid-century furnishings such as Arne Jacobsen's teak-faced Ant chair or George Nelson's colourful Marshmallow sofa.

The fluid lines of post-war furniture, crafted from materials such as plywood, laminate and tubular steel, create an organic feel, which is compounded by the addition of amoeba-shaped coffee tables and sunburst mirrors. Linear styles are also reminiscent of the period, and include sleek consoles and cabinets, and sideboards with smooth-sliding doors.

The presence of streamlined furniture works particularly well in Scandinavian-style rooms where the walls or ceiling are panelled in wood strips. Indeed, Nordic design was a major influence in fifties interiors, featuring open-plan elevations that were kitted out with blonde-wood furnishings and pale fabrics.

The inclusion of textural furnishings is another key element of fifties style, helping to soften spartan lines. To re-create the look, introduce shagpile rugs, leather upholstery and fabric lampshades. Alternatively, cover cushions with a bold floral fabric, or hang a strip of it down one wall to create an arresting focal point.

To complete the mid-century look, furnish with a selection of retro accessories. Available from antique markets and websites specializing in vintage collectibles, items include coloured glassware, bubble lamps, ball clocks and ceramics with geometric outlines.

OPPOSITE Modular furnishings, oversized florals and a shagpile rug evoke a nostalgic feel in this mid-century interior.

ABOVE RIGHT The graphic styling of a bold two-tone floral wallhanging introduces a fabulously retro feel.

PANELS & HANGINGS

Covering panels in a zany floral fabric is a great way to introduce a retro feel. If your fabric is sufficiently strong, simply staple it over a made-to-measure frame. With a less substantial fabric, the piece may need to be backed with lining. When stapling fabric onto a frame, start at the centre of one side and staple it in place, then staple the centre of the opposite side. Next staple the centre of the other two opposing sides, and work your way out to the corners, stapling on alternate sides.

✳ Choose a length of fabric – 1.5m (5ft) is a good size.

✳ Fold over the two sides and bottom edge by 5cm (2in) and hem. Fold over the top edge to make a sleeve around 4cm (1½in) deep, and stitch in place.

✳ Insert a bamboo cane into the sleeve and then tie strong cord to each end of the cane to suspend the wallhanging.

DECORATIVE DETAILS

Whether you opt for an ultra-groovy or super-sophisticated design scheme, you can be sure to find a variety of accessories to suit:

✳ **Kitsch**
Lava lamp
Beatles poster
Fibre-optic light
Litho-printed tea set
Blow-up chair
Disco ball
Plastic flowers
Target table
Pyschedelic panel
Beanbag

✳ **Cool**
Bubble TV
Andy Warhol's Flower 11 series
Verner Panton's Pantella lamp
Plywood chaise
Potted daisies
Leather cube
Monochrome print
Eero Aarnio's bubble chair

FLORALS BY MARIMEKKO

Currently enjoying a revival, furnishings by Marimekko are being snapped up by homeowners who love the vivid immediacy of its retro prints. As accessible today as they were during the 1950s, the Finnish designs are instantly recognizable, their dynamic shapes and vibrant hues fast reclaiming the number one spot for funky floral designs.

Founded in 1951 by visionary designer Armi Ratia and her husband, Viljo, Marimekko pioneered the trend for 'lifestyle' marketing, offering exuberant dress fabrics that were also used to create soft furnishing for the home. Indeed, the company's remarkable history – from its early years through to the height of its success during the 1960s and 1970s – is one of the great design success stories of the twentieth century.

These days, the reintroduction of Marimekko's classic designs has seen a further expansion into the home-furnishings market. Items such as biscuit tins and melamine plates jostle with throw pillows, shower curtains and bedlinen, while the company's trademark poppy print is available in a range of retro colours, including red and purple, yellow and orange, and black and white.

Best suited to minimalist rooms that are large enough – and light enough – to withstand the impact, Marimekko designs provide the ultimate in modern retro style.

archive florals

Although tracking down genuine wallpaper and fabrics from the sixties and seventies may take time and effort, it's perfectly possible to source retro prints from specialist shops and Internet sites selling period collectibles, such as eBay.

Often only available in one or two rolls, vintage papers are best suited to smaller rooms such as hallways, cloakrooms and dens – while rare scraps can be used to cover screens, panels and bedheads. If you want to cover a larger area, your best option is to buy a reissued print. Wallpapers by the likes of Australian designer Florence Broadhurst are now all the rage – limited editions of her famously theatrical florals grace the walls of several hip hostelries across Britain and America.

ABOVE Marimekko's coveted poppy print compounds the Scandinavian feel in this utilitarian bedroom.
OPPOSITE A panel covered with vintage wallpaper by Australian designer Florence Broadhurst provides a restrained alternative to all-over wall coverage.

OPPOSITE A floral wallhanging and selection of mid-century collectibles evoke a vintage feel in this funky home office.
LEFT Upholstering a standard-issue office chair with a retro print gives it a new lease of life.

work spaces

In the space of a single generation, computer technology has revolutionized our professional lives, allowing many of us the luxury of working at home. Not only does this offer an escape from the trials of the daily commute, but it also enables us to devise a working environment that suits our aesthetic sensibilities.

Whether you want to create a serious home office or an 'admin' corner for catching up on paperwork, retro furnishings provide an appealing combination of classic elegance and functional style. Indeed, mid-century designers such as Marcel Breuer created swivel chairs specifically for office use, while Charles and Ray Eames's steel units, complete with alternating shelves and drawers, offered the ultimate in stylish storage.

To soften the industrial lines of office furniture, introduce pattern and colour via wallpaper and upholstery. Covering office chairs with a vintage floral is an excellent way to kickstart your space, for example, while retro wallhangings introduce a homely feel. If you want to keep your walls plain, use old-fashioned papers to jazz up a variety of objects – from box files to pinboards.

It's also possible to create a mid-century look through the addition of a few key details. An Anglepoise lamp, wire wastebasket and fifties Ericofon will all help to conjure the ambience of an old-fashioned study, while a chunky schoolroom clock, wooden geometry set and seventies Date-a-Date are guaranteed to compound the vintage feel.

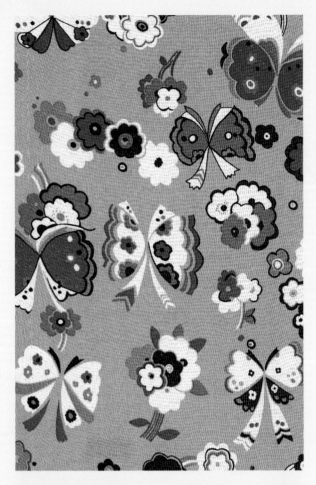

flower power

Although contemporary designers are producing a raft of funky floral motifs, nothing beats the bold blooms of the sixties and seventies. Offering a great way to kickstart neutral room schemes, the integral elements of flower power include psychedelic colours, zany wall-coverings, low-level seating and shagpile rugs. Kitsch additions such as lurid lava lamps and litho-printed ceramics complete the look.

Flowers, especially simply drawn ones, were the quintessential symbol of the sixties – appearing on fabrics, ceramics and wallpaper. Originally inspired by the hippie movement, when flowers were poked down the muzzles of guns to protest against the Vietnam war, floral motifs revolutionized home furnishings, injecting interiors with a vibrancy that had never before been witnessed.

LEFT Originally inspired by more elaborate Art Nouveau styles, sixties florals were simplified over time.
OPPOSITE A chrome table gives a mid-century feel, while the modular lamp and single floor cushion are reminiscent of sixties-style interiors.

sixties psychedelia and seventies kitsch

Taking their cue from the stylized botanicals of the Art Nouveau period, sixties florals became increasingly childlike as the decade drew on. In addition, the trend for hallucinogenic drugs resulted in an acid-bright palette and saw the emergence of floral motifs in fluorescent shades.

Perhaps the most famous flower of the day was Mary Quant's daisy, which not only appeared on all her fashion products, but also sprang up throughout the decorative arts. In addition, Quant's simple motif – a white flower on a black background – provided a graphic contrast to the brilliant blooms of Pop Art, which featured overscaled flowers that were often stylized to the point of abstraction.

Fabric designs also became bigger and brighter during the sixties. Thanks to advances in printing technology and the advent of permanent dyes, textile artists started to group brilliant colours together to dazzling effect. Favoured combinations included red and purple, orange and pink, and purple and orange, while the fashion for lime green and peony pink continued the psychedelic theme.

The trend for floral motifs and vivid colours continued well into the 1970s – together with the fashion for hippie chic. Added to the glut of brilliant blooms was a pyschedelic reworking of the classic English paisley print, which saw the signature teardrop motif being blown up to huge proportions in order to incorporate the 'lazy daisy' – a sixties favourite that remains popular to this day.

Considered by many as the decade that style forgot, the seventies witnessed an extraordinary number of aesthetic influences – from the tail end of pyschedelia to the razzle-dazzle of glam rock. Folk art was also popular, while the fashion for ethnic glitz – inspired by hippie trips to India – compounded the eclectic feel. As a result, seventies interiors featured a hotchpotch of designs, including modular furniture, shagpile carpets, tinted mirrors, lurid lampshades and sequinned floor cushions.

Towards the end of the decade, the fashion for psychedelia had given way to a softer, more neutral palette. Furnishings in mustard, avocado and chocolate brown complemented the occasional splash of brilliant tangerine, while shades of purple – including mauve, violet and lilac – reigned supreme.

LEFT Pretty floral bouquets floating on a washed-out background evoke the nostalgic appeal of days gone by.
OPPOSITE Childlike blooms in a variety of candy colours are combined with butterfly motifs to create a quirky botanical feel.

wall flowers

Bold floral wallpaper was a quintessential feature of sixties and seventies design schemes, its overscaled motifs and rich colours reflecting the ebullience of the Flower Power era. But while interiors in the 1960s featured wallpaper on all four walls, seventies-style rooms favoured a clash of different designs – including funky florals and jazzy geometrics.

Metallic wallpapers were also popular during the 1970s. Inspired by the fashion for all things disco, typical designs included plant and leaf motifs set against gold and silver backdrops. Flock wallpaper enjoyed a similar renaissance, moving from the environs of seedy nightclubs to residential room schemes. Helping to compound the trend for textural contrasts, flock provided a pleasing juxtaposition to the smoother surfaces of metal and slate.

TIP: If the impact of retro wallpaper is too dramatic for your liking, why not dilute the effect with paper cutouts? Simply find a roll of floral wallpaper or piece of vintage fabric that you like, cut out the motifs that appeal the most, and paste them onto your walls. This way, you can control the decorative impact, while still achieving a period feel. For best results, opt for florals with clear outlines in Day-Glo colours such as sunny yellows, oranges, pinks and greens. Alternatively, decorate plain walls with borders featuring sixties flowers in a range of psychedelic shades.

OPPOSITE Seventies wallpaper designs in shades of chocolate brown are still available to buy from specialist shops.
ABOVE RIGHT Floral motifs that have been cut out from retro papers and glued onto a plain background are a new spin on vintage wallcoverings, offering a restrained alternative to all-over coverage.

DECORATING WITH RETRO FLORALS

✳ Bold florals are a great way to correct a room's architectural defects as the directional stress of the pattern takes the eye beyond the flat surface of the wall, creating interest and depth.
✳ For a more sophisticated feel, contrast funky floral wallpaper with plain walls painted in complementary shades.
✳ To counter the rigid lines of modern interiors, select a softer, more fluid pattern.
✳ Use branching diagonal patterns in stairways and halls to lead the eye naturally upwards.
✳ A large pattern need not dominate the proportions of the room. Instead, choose a pale colourway to reduce the impact of an overpowering design.

✳ Using pattern successfully is all about scale and balance. If you love the texture of velvet, for example, but want to retain a light modern feel, decorate one wall with a decorative flock, which will add a period feel without completely dominating the space.
✳ Use swatches of wallpaper to jazz up functional features such as headboards and screens.
✳ To create a funky patchwork effect, use a variety of ready-made wallpaper panels and fix them onto the wall in a medley of clashing designs.
✳ Mix horizontal and vertical panels across the room and combine them with painted areas of wall to produce linear and textural contrasts.

snugs

Thanks to the availability of Modernist furnishings, it's easy to re-create a retro feel in your interiors. Better still, the graphic immediacy of decorative items from the sixties and seventies enables homeowners to introduce a sense of nostalgia – either through the inclusion of authentic vintage furnishings or via a few key accessories.

Particularly well suited to smaller sitting areas such as dens and snugs, the retro look focuses its attention on laid-back lounging. Indeed, keeping your seating sleek and streamlined is a great way to conjure the ambience of those sixties 'conversation pits', which comprised a recessed floor area surrounded by low-level seating.

Papering walls with a funky floral print is another way to evoke a vintage feel. Not for the faint-hearted, sixties and seventies wallpaper designs can be used as all-over coverage or restricted to a single 'feature' wall in order to create a striking focal point. Similarly, fabric featuring bold botanics can be used either across a variety of soft furnishings or just on a couple of cushions as a bold reminder.

Modular furniture in brightly coloured plastics is also key in retro interiors. A Panton S-chair in scorching red will complement vibrant room schemes, while the same design in white will help to create a Space Age feel. If you can't afford an original Modernist piece, introduce newly produced stacking chairs, reminiscent of original plastic designs by the likes of Robin Day and Wendell Castle.

TIP: Invariably associated with the hippie movement, burning incense is one of the easiest ways to re-create a chilled sixties vibe. For authentic aromas, opt for floral-scented incense such as jasmine, lavender, lotus flower, honeysuckle and white lilac.

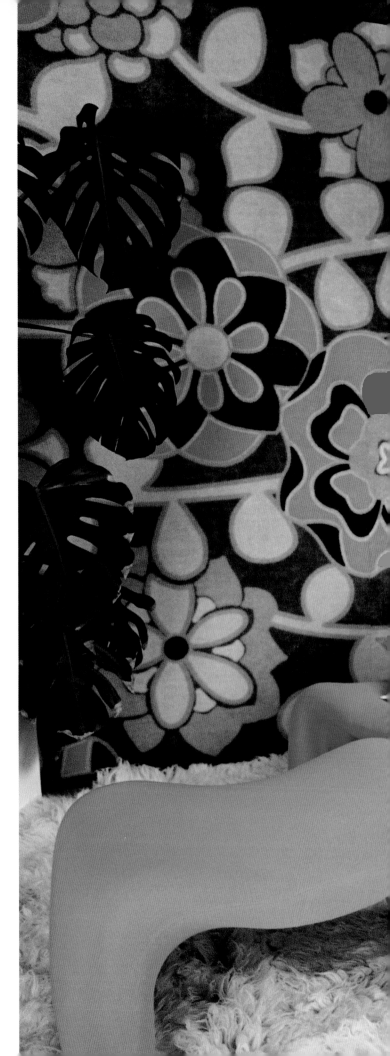

HIPPIE CHIC

Although graphic furnishings were a predominant feature in sixties and seventies interiors, the fashion for hippie chic also had a popular following. Offering a softer alternative to stark Modernist lines, the look included walls painted in saturated shades of red, green and orange, and furnishings draped with layers of ethnic fabrics. Low-level lounging was another feature of hippie interiors. Inspired by the trend for kilim floor cushions, as witnessed on travels to Morroco and Turkey, the look evolved to include all sorts of lounging options, such as bolsters, pouffes and beanbags.

These days, scattering your floor with a couple of cushions is one of the quickest and easiest ways to introduce a retro feel. If your interior has a Modernist bent, large square pillows upholstered in a bold floral will soften the effect, while those with hippie leanings should opt for oversized cushions covered in Indian block prints or Indonesian batiks. Whatever your style, make sure that your cushions are of the super-soft variety, as there's nothing remotely appealing about stiff foam fillings.

LEFT A single wall papered in graphic orange and brown florals give this snug an authentic retro feel, while the modular seating, shagpile rug and funky globe light complete the look and compound the laid-back 'loungy' vibe.

vintage florals

Timeless yet contemporary, the vintage look meshes decorative styles from the past and the present to create a cosily coherent whole. Fabulously versatile, its faded charm and sense of antiquity can be adapted to suit a variety of different dwelling places, allowing for interior schemes that look as individual as they do welcoming.

Floral fabrics, in particular, create feelings of domesticity: antique lace curtains, patchwork quilts and damask drapes create a textural warmth that is the antithesis of stark minimalism, while furniture is imbued with the rosy resonance of days gone by. In addition, although vintage style is frequently associated with cluttered maximalist interiors, it is possible to create an authentic old-fashioned feel through the inclusion of a few, carefully sourced pieces.

Whether you opt for a **MODERN ECLECTIC** look or a **CONTEMPORARY COUNTRY** one, you'll find that vintage style is attractive, informal and easy to live with. As workable in country cottages as it is in urban lofts, modern nostalgia works best in **BEDROOMS**, **DRAWING ROOMS**, **KITCHENS** and **LAUNDRY ROOMS**.

sourcing vintage florals

There can be few pursuits more rewarding than hunting for antique treasures. The frisson of excitement when you finally track down that elusive chintz-patterned teacup is unbeatable, while the expectation of stumbling across a truly original find makes the whole process doubly gratifying. Most cities and towns have salvage or junk yards, while other sources include antique markets, collectors' fairs, charity shops and car-boot sales. Local auctions present further opportunity for picking up vintage pieces, while contacting dealers whose main business is house clearance provides an excellent chance to buy job lots at knockdown prices.

Another alternative is to use the Internet, where there are numerous sites run by a variety of different antique dealers. This is a particularly good idea if you are looking for something specific, as sourcing vintage pieces electronically is obviously much quicker than trawling for treasures on foot. Surfing the Net also allows you to access dealers in other countries, enabling you to widen your search even further.

One of the reasons why decorating in vintage style is so rewarding is that the majority of items you introduce to your home are likely to be one-offs. Handcrafted collectibles, such as floral tapestries or toile candleholders, for example, are a million miles from the bland conformity of manufactured products, while sourcing sun-faded fabrics and quirky knick-knacks enables you to create interiors that resonate with authenticity.

OPPOSITE Delicate floral china is a great way of introducing a vintage feel to your interiors. Providing the perfect excuse to throw an old-fashioned tea party, floral cups and saucers also make attractive display items. For best results, showcase pretty ceramics in glass-fronted cabinets; alternatively, arrange them on Welsh dressers, so that they become an integral feature of your design scheme.

MAKE THE MOST OF ANTIQUE MARKETS

❋ Make sure that you arrive as early as possible to beat the crowds and get a good look at everything on offer.

❋ Keep an open mind: it's impossible to plan purchases in advance, so relax and go with the flow.

❋ Take cash rather than debit cards or a cheque book, as some stallholders will refuse to accept anything else. You'll also be in a better position to bargain if you're using cash.

❋ Don't forget that you can mix furniture, ornaments and fabrics from different eras and cultures.

❋ Steer clear of pieces that are badly damaged, especially if you have neither the time nor the financial resources to fix them.

❋ Very few vendors deliver, so arrange transport if you are planning to invest in some larger items.

❋ When you spot something you really like, don't let it become too obvious. Sellers immediately ask for more money if they can see that you're keen on a particular item, while other buyers may catch your enthusiasm and pip you to the post.

❋ It may take you more than one attempt to find the piece of your dreams, so persevere; it's impossible to predict what will come up for sale, and you never know when it will be your lucky day.

❋ Keep your eyes peeled for boho staples such as cane bedheads, wooden or leather trunks, sun-faded rugs and mottled mirrors.

❋ Examine vintage pieces for their previously untapped potential. For example, old window mouldings can be used to frame pictures, while black wrought-iron furniture can be instantly transformed by a lick of white paint.

modern eclectic

Decorating your space with a selection of disparate furnishings and accessories is the best way to create an interior that is both individual and appealing. Best suited to boho types, who want to produce an environment that looks like it has been casually thrown together, modern eclectic style exploits the mix-and-match effect to its maximum potential. Thus, florals are teamed with stripes, toile de Jouy is juxtaposed with gingham and bitsy buds feature alongside bold botanicals. Textural fabrics are also key in modern eclectic interiors – with old-fashioned fabrics including patchwork quilts, lace cloths, embroidered cushions and velvet drapes. Furniture-wise, choose from four-poster beds, delicate side tables and elegant chaises longues.

LEFT Blowsy rose motifs evoke a sense of days gone by.
OPPOSITE A graphic floral brightens up the mullioned window in this contemporary living room, while a mix of modern and vintage cushions helps to compound the eclectic look.

LEFT The patchwork cushions on this sofa are unified by similar colours and motifs.
OPPOSITE In order to mix different florals, ensure that your designs are alike in size and shape.

thrift florals

Recycling fabrics – either by making simple repairs or by cutting things up and making something else from them – is one of the principal pleasures of vintage style. After all, what could be more satisfying than giving a chair seat a stylish new makeover, or re-covering a lampshade with material that was once a forties tea dress?

The antithesis of today's throwaway culture, thrift crafts such as quilting and rag-rug-making have been in evidence for hundreds of years. Indeed, the practice of cobbling together fabric scraps is witnessed around the world as generations of women continue to recycle old materials in order to make new ones.

Fashionably folksy, patchwork looks particularly inviting in eclectic drawing rooms, where its homespun appeal ushers in feelings of warmth and hospitality. Used to create a variety of soft furnishings, its most popular incarnation is in the form of quilting, an age-old technique that has become an artform in America.

Although many manufacturers produce ranges of fabric especially designed for making up patchwork (some of it reproduced from old prints), the fundamental ethos of stitching scraps of material together springs from the desire to recycle and reuse. To create the most successful designs, choose textures, prints and colours that complement each other. Florals are a perennial favourite, together with checks, stripes, dots and spots. It is also possible to create an all-floral quilt, so long as you ensure that the essential element – variations on a botanical theme – remains the same. Additional fabric supplies can be sourced from dress material, damask napkins, scarves, bedlinen, tea towels, tablecloths and curtains.

Smaller pieces of velvet, brocade and satin, along with fragments of embroidery, can also be pieced together to make patchwork, either in conventional hexagon patterns or geometric blocks or, alternatively, in much more informal-looking shapes. Although patchwork quilts are usually thought of as a period bedcovering, they work equally well in vintage drawing rooms, where they can be draped over a sofa to create a colourful seat or suspended from a pole and displayed as a wallhanging.

TIP: Use fabric remnants to make pretty lavender cushions; vintage cotton florals look particularly attractive.

OPPOSITE Appliqué and lace cushions complement the wonderful toile de Jouy cover on this ornate metal bed.
RIGHT An embroidered lace and cutwork tablecloth offers the ultimate in vintage chic.

applied florals and lace

After years spent in fashion Siberia, appliqué, embroidery and knitwear have now re-entered the mainstream, thanks to fashions on the catwalk filtering down into the home. Offering a decorative alternative to minimalist materials such as leather and suede, embellished textiles are a great way to introduce an element of tactile glamour to your interior.

Whether you choose to embellish your cushions with old-fashioned pansy motifs or decorate a throw with a selection of felt flowers, the vintage drawing room is the place to do it – particularly if its main focus is a mishmash of different colours, patterns and textures. That said, decorative textiles work equally well in neutral settings, where there are fewer visual distractions. For example, a statement piece such as a single, gorgeously decorated cushion is shown off to its best advantage when it is placed on a plain divan. In the same way, larger expanses of pattern and colour – a vibrant floral throw, for example – provide the dominant focus on furniture that has been simply upholstered.

A period fabric that also manages to look perennially fashionable, lace gives vintage interiors an appealing sense of nostalgia. Available in a variety of widths and patterns – ranging from the simplest of triangles to more ornate botanically based designs – it can be as fragile as a cobweb or more opaque, as cutwork or crocheted panels. Best kept to shades of white or cream (pastels such as lavender and rose tend to look a bit sugary sweet), lace fabrics make ideal coverings for occasional tables, and can also be used as throws for the backs of sofas and chairs.

Other options for introducing this delicate fabric to your interior include lace curtains, which diffuse bright sunlight, depending on the density of the pattern; they also offer a more stylish alternative to net curtains, effectively keeping nosy neighbours at bay. You can also buy lace wallpaper, which works best in conjunction with plain furnishings. If you don't want to go the whole hog, look out for lengths of lace or crochet edging and use these to trim your cushion covers or tablecloths.

childhood, for example, or items that you have picked up while travelling abroad. By the same token, found objects such as shells, stones, leaves and feathers will also strike an authentic note, thanks to their intrinsic beauty and sense of organic naturalism.

Combining objects to create an attractive display involves a good deal of trial and error; helpful pointers include grouping together objects from a similar period – even when they're made from very different materials – or opting for bizarre juxtapositions in which disparate groups of items are featured. For example, coloured glassware, an antique figurine, silver snuff boxes and a wind-up toy will all give vintage-style drawing rooms a historical feel.

Objects that make you smile are a must. An old Coronation mug filled with a blowsy hydrangea makes much more of a statement than a cut-glass vase filled with two dozen carnations, for instance, while a whimsical china animal or a souvenir wedding plate adds a kitsch element that rarely goes amiss. It's also possible to lighten the appearance of heavyweight antiques with playful additions such as a string of floral fairylights draped over a sombre oil painting or a saucy postcard tucked inside a gilt frame.

When it comes to eclectic displays, the most important thing to remember is not to go overboard. Too many decorative pieces – however pleasing they may be individually – will cause visual mayhem when they're bunched together. Instead, restrict yourself to a few cleverly composed vignettes – especially in rooms of a minimalist nature.

timeworn treasures

Displays of objects are a significant feature of vintage interiors, offering yet another opportunity to stamp rooms with a sense of personal history. Predictably, there are few rules about what to include and what not, although the quirkier and more eclectic your collection, the better. It's also advisable to remember that off-beat items are particularly well suited to vintage interiors – as the general effect is greater than the sum of its parts.

One of the best ways to create an intriguing display is to ensure that you only include objects that speak to your heart – relics from your

ABOVE LEFT A collection of painted and gilded antique glass containers conjures up a superb sense of nostalgia.
OPPOSITE Vintage trimmings spilling out of a rose-patterned box are reminiscent of an old-fashioned haberdashery.

'EVERYTHING'S COMING UP ROSES.' Stephen Sondheim, songwriter

bedrooms

The modern eclectic interior borrows from a wide variety of sources to create a style that is as adventurous as it is colourful. Particularly well suited to lush bedrooms, where exquisite textiles in life-affirming colours can be displayed to their maximum potential, the focus is on a mish-mash of styles and traditions – as opposed to a glut of themed collections.

The best way to create a boho boudoir is to combine antique furniture styles with modern ones: a 70-30 mix works well, as long as you make sure that the majority of pieces are in the contemporary mould, as this will enable you to create a unique decorative scheme rather than a pastiche of a period interior. It's also possible to strike a balance between old and new by teaming nineteenth-century floral paintings with modern photographs, or accessorizing a spanking new bedspread with a selection of endearingly threadbare cushions.

Vintage fabrics work especially well in bedrooms, thanks to their old-fashioned allure and softly-softly approach. In addition, there is an intriguing heritage of antique textiles available – from Victorian chintzes to pretty embroidery and stylized sixties blooms.

For best results, combine florals with contemporary furniture for a modern-country feel, or create a cottage-garden look by setting spriggy prints against a bright white background. Sensuous fabrics such as velvet, satin, chintz, lace and organza evoke a sense of glamour and romance, while textiles that are embroidered, appliquéd or made from patchwork give a fashionable folksy feel.

RIGHT The clever use of luxuriant fabrics and rich colours creates an atmosphere that is stylishly eccentric rather than garish and overdone, while the modern-vintage mix compounds the uniquely glamorous feel.

'I HAVE NO RECIPE FOR HOW TO COMBINE THINGS. BUT YOU MUST BE SINCERE.

AND IF YOU ARE, STRANGELY, IT WILL SUCCEED.' Andrée Putman, interior designer

mixing and matching

The bedroom is the most indulgent room in the home, and provides the perfect space for allowing your floral fantasies to run free. Indeed, there are few limits to how many patterns you include, as long as you focus your attention on a single area. Layers of floral prints look effective on beds, for example, offering a funkier, more flexible alternative to full sets of matching sheets and pillows, but remember to create a calming balance; after all, this is supposed to be a place of rest.

To mix and match bedclothes successfully, you need to ensure that everything else in the room is kept neutral. By removing, editing and simplifying the rest of your décor, fabrics are able to reign supreme. A group of textiles need not share a common date or origin, provided the patterns have a resonance among themselves. Better still, mixing and matching patterns offers the chance to create exciting compositions full of dramatic changes in scale and outline; it also means that old and new can be combined to give your boudoir a truly individual feel.

What goes well together is not an exact science, but similar colours and shades – as well as related motifs – are good starting points. To prevent confusion, choose a selection of designs that are alike in terms of colour, mood or type, but steer clear of similarity in size. One may be multi-coloured, another feature a dominant colour from the first together with white, and a third display a duet of two-toning shades.

You can also mix and match designs from different eras, provided you stick to a common colour theme, as too many different shades can make a room appear overly busy. To avoid a cluttered Victorian look – or clashing pattern overload – ensure that you mix only prints and designs that fall within a similar colour range, and that the rest of your décor – including floors and walls – is kept as neutral as possible.

Although you can use any sort of floral patterns for your boho bed, the vintage look undoubtedly works best. Sun-faded fabrics that have seen some wear and tear complement each other far better than brand new ones, for example, while the bright hues of funky florals can appear garish and over-bright.

As far as cushion covers are concerned, why not put different designs on each side? A bold chintz combined with a striking plaid, for example, provides double the decorative choice, as well as an element of the unexpected.

> **TIP:** Do practise some restraint on the mix and match front, or your room may end up looking like it belongs to an old lady.

OPPOSITE Mix vintage fabrics from the same period to create an easy sense of coherence.

ABOVE Juxtaposing floral fabrics with striped ones remains a perennially popular decorating technique.

drawing rooms

The key to creating a modern eclectic look is to ensure that your lounging area is as comfortable as it is stylish. There is no point in creating a showcase brimming with vintage finds and then discovering that it's too rarified to actually kick back and relax in. This is a particularly salient point as regards vintage-style drawing rooms, which should aim to combine comfort and accessibility with flair and individuality.

Luckily, this approach sums up the essence of vintage style, where the main focus is placed on cosy, timeworn furnishings that are also easy on the eye. After all, what could be more appealing than a huge squashy sofa, upholstered with a unique floral throw, or an alluring window seat, scattered with a raggle-taggle of mismatched cushions?

Because they tend to be larger than other rooms in the house, drawing rooms provide an excellent domain for the modern eclectic look. Spacious enough to accommodate a hotchpotch of furniture, ornaments and fabrics from different eras and cultures, their décor should be viewed as something that evolves slowly and enjoyably over many years.

To create a truly successful vintage interior, patience is paramount. Although there are no hard and fast rules, it is vital to remember that the main criteria for choosing vintage furnishings and accessories are that you love the way they look and will enjoy living with them. Understandably, accumulating such a collection of heart-felt treasures takes time, but the end result – a genuinely nostalgic room that reverberates with a sense of history – is undoubtedly worth the wait.

RIGHT The charming appeal of this vintage drawing room is based on its eclectic furnishings, old-fashioned upholstery and quirky decorative accessories, including a wooden stepladder and an antique set of weighing scales.

FURNISHING WITH OLD-FASHIONED FABRICS

Vintage fabrics play a key role in the decoration of eclectic drawing rooms, introducing a timeless quality that ushers in feelings of warmth and integrity. As a general rule, the most attractive fabrics are those that are already a little worn-in: a splashy Art Nouveau pattern, for example, looks more appealing if the colours are slightly sun-bleached, while a patched and darned chair cover adds an unbeatable feeling of immutability.

The sense of exclusivity that is a by-product of antique textiles adds to their charm. Hand-woven fabrics, in particular, are becoming increasingly hard to track down – as well as being expensive. Thus, it is important to remember that even the smallest scraps can be used to evoke a sense of nostalgia – as covers for precious books, for example. Similarly, if you find a small piece of fabric you long to turn into a duvet cover, enlarge it with a border in a complementary fabric to make up the extra.

Sometimes, it's impossible to find the exact pattern you're looking for, however hard you search. If this is the case, why not opt for a reproduction print? Available in a wide choice of patterns, modern materials decorated with vintage designs are almost as good as the real thing – particularly if the manufacturer has artificially aged the fabric by adjusting the dyes and chemical solutions.

contemporary country

Chic, simple and uncomplicated, contemporary country style celebrates the homespun pleasures of bygone days in a thoroughly modern way. Providing a welcome escape from the techno-wizardry of twenty-first-century life, the look is fabulously rustic, while still retaining a good degree of comfort and decoration.

As befits all vintage interiors, furnishings that have seen some action are a key feature. A pine dining table with a well-scrubbed surface, or a paint-chipped dresser or cabinet compound the sense of nostalgia, while a palette of pale colours provides the perfect backdrop for a variety of floral media – from spriggy wallpaper to blowsy ceramics.

LEFT Brightly coloured florals set against a dazzling white background evoke a charming country-cottage feel.
OPPOSITE The pale décor and panelled walls of this country kitchen are a perfect canvas for modern rustic additions such as roughly painted chairs and an eclectic mix of fabrics.

LEFT Floral wallpaper is a key feature in rustic interiors, while a selection of fashionable accessories adds a modern feel.

OPPOSITE All-white furnishings — with just a hint of floral detail — create a sense of serenity.

the rustic look

To create a rural-looking interior, it's important that you make sure your walls and floors are as natural looking as possible. Luckily, this is pretty straightforward, thanks to the availability of a wide variety of old-fashioned paint finishes, which help to evoke a bucolic sense of space and calm. If you want your walls to have a rough-and-ready feel, for example, try traditional distemper, which gives a pleasantly chalky finish; for surfaces that look elegantly flat, use limewash, while the natural pigments in casein milk paint give a soft pastel hue.

Floral wallpaper is another staple in rustic interiors, providing the perfect cover-up for walls that are covered in lumps, bumps and unsightly marks. Opt for old-fashioned prints to continue the vintage theme, or choose practical, wipe-clean vinyl papers, which come in a wide range of colours and patterns and will give functional rooms such as kitchens, bathrooms and laundry rooms a pretty, decorative feel.

For woodwork, try flat oil paint, which gives a very matte finish, or more durable oil eggshell,

which has the advantage of marking less easily, but does have a slight sheen. If you're planning a rustic room from scratch, it is advisable to pick a paint that goes with your chosen fabric choice (you can always get emulsion specially mixed to the shade you require), rather than trying to find a fabric that matches your choice of paint colour.

Although simply furnished modern-rustic interiors tend to feel calm and uncluttered, this does not mean that you should restrict yourself to a bland palette of white or off-white. Instead, opt for rich earthy shades of terracotta, brick, ochre and moss green, which will complement rugged country furnishings and evoke a reassuring, lived-in feel. Alternatively, choose lighter floral-inspired hues that are reminiscent of summer gardens: the delicate shades of lavender, clematis and buddleia are all wonderfully subtle, and work much better than stronger colours, which are too overpowering for the majority of rustic room schemes.

THIS PAGE A wall stencil is given a contemporary twist by extending across the glass-fronted cabinet, and onto the floor in front of it. OPPOSITE Delicate furniture and vintage accessories create the perfect complement to the pale décor of this ethereal kitchen.

In keeping with the back-to-basics look, rustic-style floors are durable and down to earth. Choose neutral carpets or sisal matting if you want to ensure that your interior remains cosy throughout the winter months, or cover brick, slate or stone-flagged floors with floral rugs to introduce warmth, pattern and colour.

Stripped wooden floorboards also evoke the timeless appeal of country life, and can be employed in a number of ways to create different looks within the home. Use them on your floors, walls and ceilings to imitate the intimacy of a cosy log cabin, or limewash dark boards to open up small rooms by creating a feeling of lightness and expansion. The streamlined appearance of stripped boards also works brilliantly with wooden furniture that's been carved from a different grain, providing a pleasing textural contrast that is naturally spontaneous.

Floral floor stencils are another option in rustic interiors, providing an arty feel that suits the pastoral profile. Easy to apply, as well as being inexpensive and fabulously low maintenance, stencils should be painted onto sanded floors, and then covered with several coats of polyurethane, to ensure that they withstand years of wear and tear.

Wood furniture is an integral part of country interiors, helping to promote feelings of warmth and longevity. Easily sourced from antique shops and flea markets, traditional wood furnishings are solid and practical (although not necessarily lacking in decoration), while the warm patina of old timber evokes a mellow ambience – as well as providing an attractive contrast to newer, sleeker styles.

It's also important to note that different types of wood summon different atmospheres. If you want to create a calming feel, for example, opt for pale, light-reflecting timbers such as bleached driftwood or golden pine. A homely ambience is best achieved with richly coloured grains such as cherry, while dark woods including stained oak or gleaming ebony are guaranteed to promote feelings of intimacy and seclusion.

Painted wooden furniture is another option, imbuing interiors with a naïve, homely feel. Particularly well suited to modern design schemes, it effectively masks any defficiencies in the wood, in addition to helping small dark rooms appear bigger and brighter. For best effects, opt for distressed pieces, where the grain can be spotted beneath layers of peeling paint.

TIP: To make sure that you're buying genuine vintage fabric, check for authentic signs of ageing, such as fading along fold marks.

showcase florals

Pretty displays of floral china are one of the keynotes of modern country kitchens, instilling them with sense of style and individuality. Better still, building up a collection of crockery – be it a matching set or an eclectic one – is an enjoyably slow process that involves lots of antique shopping and can take years to complete.

Another advantage of collecting china is the fact that it's still possible to buy tableware from markets and thrift shops at gratifyingly low prices. Single plates are particularly inexpensive, for instance, as well as being relatively easy to come by. If you're planning to build up a dinner service using second-hand ceramics, however, it's important that you scan potential purchases for chips and cracks, which will obviously render some pieces unusable.

Even if crockery appears to be in mint condition, keep your eyes peeled as it may have been 'invisibly' restored. (Repaired cracks are painted over with a matte white finish and can be very easy to miss unless you know what to look for.) Restored china cannot be used on a day-to-day basis, as repeated washing will cause the glue to dissolve. If you use these pieces for display purposes only, however, the odd crack or chip will compound the vintage effect nicely.

In order to show off ceramics to their best advantage, choose glass-fronted cabinets and dressers, which have been especially designed for display purposes. Alternatively, store your china in elegant armoires, and leave the doors ajar to reveal stacks of pretty plates. It's also possible to showcase your crockery on a Welsh dresser – a country-kitchen staple that provides open and closed storage for tableware.

If you don't have room for a full-size dresser, or even one of the smaller versions, customize your own display area with a rack or a set of open shelves fixed to the wall. These can be made from reclaimed floorboards, or any piece of wood that looks suitably rough-hewn. If you're pushed for space, attach small hooks to the underside of shelves to hang mugs, jugs and utensils such as cheese graters and sieves.

Mixing different styles of china on shelves and dressers is an integral part of vintage style, reinforcing the notion that, although practicality is paramount, décor also has a part to play. White or off-white walls are the best backgrounds for displaying a collection of ceramics, while mismatched pieces introduce an informal feel.

For the most spontaneous displays (and therefore the most effective), simply select those pieces that you love the most and place them alongside other items that also speak to your soul. For best results, mix old styles with newer ones, rather than sticking to pieces of the same vintage. In addition, objects that create a stunning visual surprise – a plain purple jug among a clutch of primrose patterned plates, for example – will pump up the pace in an instant.

Contrasting textures is another display technique, and could include the arrangement of delicate chintz designs on rough, chunky shelving, for example, or glossy Art Deco florals set against roughly distempered walls. It's also advisable to try and balance larger pieces with smaller ones; this way, you will avoid the mind-numbing uniformity that's guaranteed to kill ceramic displays stone dead.

If the haphazard look is too disorganized for your liking, one solution is to theme different pieces to create a more coherent effect: a mass of unmatched cream and white chinaware looks coolly coordinated, for instance.

TIP: Remove stains from vintage china by soaking it thoroughly in a bucket of cool, diluted washing powder.

OPPOSITE Plates and dishes patterned with old-fashioned florals give this kitchen a unique sense of character.

kitchens

Warm, friendly and inviting, kitchens are fast replacing dining rooms as the most conducive of places to eat and entertain. No longer viewed as cold and impersonal spaces, the modern kitchen has become a social hub where family and friends gather to pass the time of day. Particularly suited to country-style kitchens, this trend reflects the ancient farmhouse tradition in which the kitchen is the beating heart of the home.

As suited to urban spaces as it is to rural ones, the country-style kitchen is witnessed throughout the Western world – with designs ranging from minimalist Scandinavian styles to elegant French farmhouse ones. The common denominator is the sense of warmth and nostalgia, which can be as easily manifested in a high-rise flat as it is in a converted barn.

Décor-wise, simplicity is key. To establish a traditional feel, consider installing an enamel-fronted cooker or Aga, which will keep your kitchen toasty throughout the year. Scour your local salvage yard for period fixtures and fittings such as a deep ceramic sink, a butcher's block, reclaimed taps and rough-hewn floorboards, which make excellent rustic shelves.

Lighting is another way to create an inviting atmosphere in country-style kitchens. For best results, look for styles that will efficiently illuminate working areas, and combine with table and floor lamps for more relaxed spots. You should also incorporate lighting that is flexible enough to cope with a variety of dining situations – from raucous parties to cosy twosomes. If you choose pendant lights to illuminate your table, use tungsten bulbs, which emit a soft creamy glow.

The centrepiece of any country kitchen is the table. For the ultimate bucolic look, choose an old refectory style or an antique pine job with a battle-scarred surface. Storage should be similarly olde-worlde: eschew bland, fitted units in favour of freestanding pieces that have seen some service: stripped pine cupboards and scrubbed wooden dressers are so much more appealing than laminated counters and smooth-sliding drawers, while open shelves piled with floral crockery will compound the free-and-easy feel.

Even if your kitchen is on the small side, it's still possible to create a rustic look by incorporating concealed storage. This will keep the dull stuff out of sight and allow for a display of pastoral paraphernalia. A combination of built-in units with an old-fashioned plate rack strikes the right note, for example, while a melange of old-fashioned utensils hanging from ceiling hooks, or pots of herbs on your windowsill, continues the theme.

It also helps to think laterally when it comes to kitting out your kitchen. For example, a cosy armchair could be transferred from the sitting room to a niche by the stove, or a chest of drawers moved from the bedroom to serve as storage space for kitchen utensils.

Fabric is an effective way to soften the utilitarian lines of kitchen cabinets, as well as introducing a secondary colour to your cooking area. For a truly vintage effect, hang a floral curtain beneath the sink to hide ugly plumbing. Alternatively, employ floral 'skirts' to disguise modern monstrosities such as dishwashers, tumble driers and freezer cabinets. Kitchens are full of steamy aromas, so make sure that soft furnishings such as curtains, blinds or chair covers can be washed. By the same token, avoid displaying valuable artworks in your cooking area; instead, decorate walls with floral prints, tiles and decorative plates.

OPPOSITE A faded tablecloth, some quirky decoration and a mish-mash of different furnishing styles create a homely feel in this charmingly cluttered kitchen.

TEN WAYS TO ADD FLORALS TO KITCHENS

Although today's kitchens are full of gadgets, it's possible to counter the hi-tech look with an assortment of floral details:

✽ Hang café curtains from a stretched wire to create a funky fifties feel.

✽ Employ a similar technique to keep unattractive white goods such as your dishwasher or tumble drier hidden from view.

✽ Enliven a drab corner with an arrangement of floral tiles, which are as practical as they are pretty.

✽ Reupholster stool seats with petal-patterned pads, and brighten up dining chairs with mix-and-match squab cushions tied onto the back struts (this is also an excellent way of using up smaller pieces of vintage fabrics).

✽ Make an assortment of napkins from vintage scraps, or use off-cuts to trim plain tablemats.

✽ Line the backs of cupboards, kitchen shelves and cutlery drawers with floral wallpaper or thickly waxed floral giftwrap.

✽ Recycle a twenties tea dress to make a noughties apron.

✽ Rugs are a good way of introducing a floral theme, but make sure that they are made from material that can be easily cleaned, as spillages are bound to occur.

✽ Introduce florals via kitchen basics such as tea towels, oven gloves, pot stands and place mats.

✽ Decorate your windowsill with a heavenly scented hyacinth or a row of jaunty geraniums.

A far cry from the rigorous style of minimalist cooking zones, where everything is hidden behind brushed-steel units, vintage kitchens feature an exuberant mix of free-standing furniture, fabrics and utensils. Abundance is the name of the game, here, and the fruitful look is compounded by a celebration of nature. Thus, a bowl brimming with speckled eggs is proudly exhibited alongside a pot of basil, while a basket of apples is displayed next to a trug brimming with wild flowers.

Although the inclusion of numerous objects is a key feature in vintage kitchens, it should be noted that many of the decorative items you choose to showcase have an intrinsic beauty that's born out of years of hard graft. For example, a collection of old-fashioned ladles, whisks and wooden spoons bunched together in a floral pot is both attractive and functional, while gleaming copper saucepans suspended from the ceiling are as necessary as they are aesthetic.

Although vintage kitchenware has been popular for quite some time, there is still plenty of it around to buy. Best sourced from flea markets, antique shops and car boot sales, where vendors are likely to give good deals, many of the kitchenware items are likely to show a degree of wear and tear. This should not present any real problems, however, as chips and scratches bear witness to past times when life seemed simpler and less fraught than it does today.

Old-fashioned gadgets are another way of giving rustic kitchens a vintage feel. Early versions of coffee grinders, nutcrackers, cheese graters, whisks and weighing scales provide an authentic look. Similarly, patterned antiques such as battered rose-patterned cake tins and old tea caddies combine with enamel colanders, French storage jars and pestle and mortars to complete the nostalgic theme.

The modern rustic kitchen is rarely complete without the addition of a few loosely informal flower arrangements. For best results, fill your space with typical country blooms such as poppies, black-eyed Susans, sunflowers, hollyhocks or cow parsley. To complete the look, requisition kitchen containers as an alternative to conventional glass or ceramic vases. Items such as milk jugs, tin cans, storage jars and tumblers are perfect for simple blooms, while cast-iron buckets and enamel coffee pots are suitable for bolder arrangements.

TIP: Old-fashioned French armoires with door panels faced in chicken wire provide a perfect frame for floral fabrics, which can be tacked onto battens set inside the door. If you have ordinary wooden cupboards, simply remove the centre section of the front panel and replace it with wire mesh to create the same effect.

OPPOSITE A floral-print apron provides the perfect finishing touch in this wonderful green and pink kitchen.
ABOVE Floral blinds backed with a contrasting checked fabric soften harsh edges and introduce a relaxed feel.

laundry rooms

Thanks to their associations with age-softened sheets and embroidered lavender sachets, laundry rooms have an inherent vintage feel and provide the perfect forum for showing off your finest floral fabrics. After all, what could look more attractive than pretty piles of vintage eiderdowns, petal-patterned pillowcases, blooming curtains and sprigged sheets?

Traditionally a female domain, laundry rooms emanate a sense of purity that inspires a decorative scheme that is light, bright and pretty. If your space is on the small side, paper the walls with darling buds, which work better in more compact rooms; alternatively, line shelves with floral paper, or transform vintage fabrics into covers for ironing boards and coat hangers. You can also stitch together a variety of cloth bags from old-fashioned scraps and use them for storing pegs and odd socks.

> **TIP:** To scent linen naturally, add a solution of a clear essential oil, such as lavender, to the final rinse in the washing machine.

ABOVE A floral ironing board enlivens a utility room.

OPPOSITE Laundry bags provide a pretty alternative to dull linen baskets and are a decorative device in their own right.

STORING VINTAGE FABRICS

❋ Fabrics that are not in frequent use should be stored somewhere dark and dry. If you don't have a linen cupboard, a chest of drawers is a good substitute.
❋ Line shelves or drawers with paper so the fabric doesn't come into contact with the wood.
❋ Wrap delicate fabrics in acid-free tissue paper and gently roll them up to avoid straining the fibres.
❋ Do not use airing cupboards for storage. Instead, store vintage fabrics in cardboard boxes and make sure they are kept dry.
❋ Do not use plastic boxes for storage; the air cannot circulate, which might encourage mildew.
❋ To keep stored fabrics fresh, tie a handful of potpourri into an old floral handkerchief, and hang your makeshift bag inside the linen cupboard door.

IRONING-BOARD COVER

Take the drudgery out of ironing with floral ironing-board covers, which are simple and easy to make:
❋ To turn your ironing board into a decorative feature rather than a dreaded object, recycle an old floral fabric to use as your cover, bearing in mind that a heavyweight cotton will last longer.
❋ Make sure you use flameproof lining and check the fabric does not have any manmade content, which could be flammable.
❋ Trace the pattern from the old cover, and add a drawstring so that it's easy to take off to wash.

address book

ALTFIELD
2/22 Chelsea Harbour Design
Centre, London SW10 0XE
020 7351 5893
www.altfield.com
*Chinese lamps, silk cushions, screens,
wallpaper panels.*

AMANDA ROSS
Studio 54, Clink Studios, 1 Clink
Street, London SE1 9DG
020 7234 0832
*Hand-printed silk cushions and
decorative wall panels.*

ANDREW MARTIN
200 Walton Street, London SW3 2JL
020 7225 5100
www.andrewmartin.co.uk
*Fabrics, trimmings, wallpapers,
furniture and accessories.*

ANNA FRENCH
343 Kings Road, London SW3 5ES
020 7351 1126
www.annafrench.co.uk
*Fabric, lace and wallpaper, plus
decorative accessories such as rose-
shaped fairylights.*

ARTCO
1 Meanwood Close, Leeds,
West Yorkshire LS7 2JF
Tel: 0113 262 0056
www.artco.co.uk
*Modern art, with over 250 paintings
available to buy.*

BAER & INGRAM
Dragon Works, Leigh on Mendip,
Radstock BA3 5QZ
01373 813 800.
www.baer-ingram.com
*Country-style furniture, patchwork
quilts, wallpaper, bed and bathware.*

BENNISON FABRICS
16 Holbein Place, London SW1W 8NL
020 7730 8076

www.bennisonfabrics.com
*King of muted eighteenth-century-
style fabrics.*

BOOM! INTERIORS
115–17 Regents Park Road,
London NW1 8UR
020 7722 6622
www.boominteriors.com
*Original twentieth-century furniture,
plus modern art and design.*

CABBAGES & ROSES
3 Langton Street, London SW10 0JL
020 7352 7333
Mail order: 01225 859 151
www.cabbagesandroses.com
*Faded floral linens, vintage
accessories.*

CATH KIDSTON
51 Marylebone High Street,
London W1U 5HW
020 7935 6555
Mail order: 020 7229 8000
www.cathkidston.co.uk.
*Painted furniture, fifties-inspired
vintage and modern fabrics,
wallpapers and accessories.*

CHELSEA TEXTILES
13 Walton Street, London SW3 2JD
020 7584 5544
www.chelseatextiles.com
*Faithful re-creations of antique
textiles, cushions and furnishings.*

COEXISTENCE
288 Upper Street, London N1 2TZ
020 7354 8817
www.coexistence.co.uk
*Represents 100 manufacturers of
furniture, lighting and accessories.*

COLEFAX AND FOWLER
110 Fulham Road, London SW3 6HU
020 7244 7427
*Essential English furnishing fabrics
and wallpapers.*

**THE CURTAIN
EXCHANGE**
129–31 Stephendale Road,
London SW6 2PF
020 7731 8316
www.thecurtainexchange.co.uk
*Bespoke and ready-made curtains and
blinds, plus second-hand curtains.*

DESIGNERS GUILD
267 & 277 Kings Road,
London SW3 5EN
020 7351 5775
www.designersguild.com
*Modern furniture and fabrics
including designs by Jasper Conran,
Emily Todhunter and Ralph Lauren.*

ENGLISH HOME
The Old Warehouse, 2 Michael
Road, LondonSW6 2AD
020 7384 3020
www.englishhome.com
Cushions, bedcovers and curtains.

EW MOORE & SON
39–43 Plashet Grove,
London E6 1AD
020 8471 9392
www.ewmoore.com
*Vintage wallpaper from the 1960s
to the 1980s.*

HABITAT
196 Tottenham Court Road,
London W1P 9LD
020 7631 3880
For branches calls: 0845 601 0740
www.habitat.co.uk
*Modern furniture, furnishings
lighting and home accessories.*

HARVEY MARIA
17 Riverside Business Park, Lyon
Road, London SW19 2RL
020 8542 0088
www.harveymaria.co.uk
*Vinyl tiles depicting a variety of
photographic images.*

**JANE CHURCHILL
INTERIORS**
81 Pimlico Road, London SW1W 8PH
020 7730 8564
www.janechurchillinteriors.com
*Traditional English country-house
fabrics and furnishings.*

JOHN LEWIS
Oxford Street, London W1A 1EX
020 7629 7711
www.johnlewis.com
Enormous range of fabrics.

**JUDY GREENWOOD
ANTIQUES**
657–9 Fulham Road,
London SW6 5PY
020 7736 6037
*Antique cushions, quilts and
tapestries.*

THE LAUNDRY
PO Box 22007, London SW2 1WU
020 7274 3838
*Mail order 1930s–1950s-inspired
patterned bedlinen.*

LAURA ASHLEY
256–8 Regent Street,
London W1L 5DA
020 7437 9760
For a catalogue call: 08712 302 301
www.lauraashley.com
*Classic floral furnishing fabrics,
wallpapers and accessories.*

LEPORELLO
PO Box 68, East Horsley,
Surrey KT24 6YT
01483 284 109
www.leporello.co.uk
Hand-painted rustic style furniture.

LIBERTY
Regent Street, London W1B 5AH
020 7734 1234
www.liberty.co.uk
Old-fashioned floral fabrics.

LOMBOK
204–8 Tottenham Court Road,
London W1T 7LJ
020 7580 0800
www.lombok.co.uk
Furnishings from the Far East.

MARIMEKKO
16–17 St Christopher's Place,
London W1U 1NZ
020 7486 6454
www.marimekko.co.uk
Bold Finnish textiles and accessories.

MEGAN PARK
65 Leonard Street, London EC2A 4QS
020 7739 5828
www.meganpark.co.uk
Embroidered homeware.

MISSONI HOME
Interdesign UK, G30 Chelsea Design
Centre, London SW10 0XE
020 7376 5272
www.missonihome.com
Brightly coloured homeware.

MULBERRY HOME
322 Kings Road, London SW3 5UH
020 7823 3455
www.mulberry.com
Richly textured furnishing fabrics.

NEISHA CROSLAND
8 Elystan Street, London SW3 3NS
020 7584 7988
www.neishacrosland.com
*Inspiratational print-based
furnishings and fabrics.*

NINA CAMPBELL
9 Walton Street, London SW3 2JW
020 7225 1011
www.ninacampbell.com
Furnishings, fabrics and wallpapers.

ORNAMENTA
020 7591 0077
www.ornamenta.co.uk

*Hand-printed wallpaper and site-
specific designs by Jane Gordon Clark.*

OSBORNE & LITTLE
304 Kings Road, London SW3 5UH
020 7352 1456
www.osborneandlittle.com
*Leading designer of English country-
house fabric and wallpapers.*

PAINT & PAPER LIBRARY
5 Elystan Street, London SW3 3NT
020 7581 1075
Mail order: 020 7823 7755
www.paintlibrary.co.uk
Modern paints and wallpapers.

PLANET BAZAAR
397 St John Street, London EC1V 4LD
020 7278 7793
www.planetbazaar.co.uk
*Original twentieth-century furniture
and lighting, and Pop art accessories.*

RACHEL KELLY
71 Goldman Close, London E2 6EF
020 729 3552
www.interactivewallpaper.co.uk
*Interactive wallpaper; customers
can tailor-make their own designs.*

RALPH LAUREN HOME
1 New Bond Street, London W1S 3RL
020 7535 4600
www.polo.com
*Designer homeware including a
wide range of bedlinen.*

ROMO
Lowmoor Road, Kirkby in Ashfield,
Nottinghamshire NG17 7DE
01623 756699
www.romofabrics.com
*Modern floral fabrics in sumptuous
silk, satin, linen and cotton.*

THE RUG COMPANY
124 Holland Park Avenue,
London W11 4UE

020 7229 5148
www.therugcompany/info
*Designer rugs by Paul Smith, Diana
von Furstenberg and Matthew
Williamson, among others.*

SCALAMANDRÉ
G/4 Chelsea Harbour Design
Centre, London SW10 0XE
020 7795 0988
www.scalamandre.com
Printed and silk furnishing fabrics.

SERA OF LONDON
020 7286 5923
www.seraoflondon.com
*Interior design service, plus luxury
homeware.*

SHABBY CHIC
1013 Montana Avenue,
Santa Monica, CA 90403, USA
+1 310 394 1975
www.shabbychic.com
*Classic country-style floral fabrics,
bedlinen and accessories.*

SHARLAND AND LEWIS
52 Long Street, Tetbury,
Gloucestershire GL8 8AQ
01666 500 354
www.sharlandandlewis.com
*Rustic furnitue, antique linens,
decorative accessories.*

SKANDIUM
86 Marylebone High Street,
London W1U 4QS
020 7935 2077
www.skandium.com
*Modern Scandinavian furniture,
kitchenware and textiles.*

STENCIL LIBRARY
Stocksfield Hall, Stocksfield,
Northumberland NE43 7TN
01661 844 844
www.stencil-library.com
Huge range of pre-cut stencils.

SVENSKT TENN
Strandvägen 5, Box 5478,
SE-11484 Stockholm, Sweden
+46 8 670 16 00
www.svenskttenn.se
*Swedish design company selling
textiles furniture and lamps.*

TAPETTITALO
Fleminginkatu 4, 00530 Helsinki,
Finland
+358 9 76 76 58
www.tapettitalo.fi
*Finnish purveyors of over 200
Scandinavian wallpapers.*

TIMOROUS BEASTIES
384 Great Western Road,
Glasgow G4 9HT, Scotland
0141 337 2622
www.timorousbeasties.com
*Funky fabrics, roller blinds,
wallpapers and accessories.*

TOBIAS & THE ANGEL
66–8 White Hart Lane,
London SW13 0PZ
020 8878 8902
www.tobiasandtheangel.com
*A treasure-trove of new and vintage
homeware.*

TORD BOONTJE
The Bake House, Basing Court,
16a Peckham High Street,
London SE15 5DT
020 7732 6460
www.tordboontje.com
*Modern furnishings including
lighting, embroidered chairs, paper
screens and digital-print fabrics.*

VV ROULEAUX
6 Marylebone High Street,
London W1M 3PB
020 7224 5179
www.vvrouleaux.com
*Ribbons, trimmings, braid and
couture flowers.*

index

Figures in italics refer to captions.

acknowledgments

The publisher would like to thank the following photographers, agencies and companies for their kind permission to reproduce the following photographs in this book:

2 Bill Kingston/Elle Decoration; 5 Courtesy of Romo Fabrics; 6 Mark Williams/Elle Decoration; 9 Courtesy of Osborne & Little; 10–11 Courtesy of Cath Kidston Ltd; 12 Lars Ranek; 14 above Courtesy of Cath Kidston Ltd; 14 below Courtesy of The Curtain Exchange; 15 Courtesy of Designers Guild; 16 Mel Yates/Elle Decoration; 16–17 Tom Leighton/Homes & Gardens/IPC Syndication; 18 Caroline Arber/Homes & Gardens/IPC Syndication; 19 Annika Vannerus; 20 Tom Leighton/Homes & Gardens/IPC Syndication; 21 Courtesy of Romo Fabrics; 22 Alex Sarginson; 23 Gaelle le Boulicaut; 24 Simon Brown/Red Cover; 25 Mikkel Vang; 26 Lina Ikse Bergman/Elle Decoration; 27 Polly Wreford/Living Etc/IPC Syndication; 28 Gaelle le Boulicaut; 29 Minh + Wass (Designer: Betsey Johnson); 30 left Jan Baldwin/Narratives; 30–1 Pia Tryde/Courtesy of Cath Kidston Ltd; 32 Kim Sayer/Homes & Gardens/IPC Syndication; 33 Deborah Jaffe; 34 above Courtesy of Cath Kidston Ltd; 34 below Courtesy of Cabbages and Roses; 35 Dennis Brandsma/VT Wonen/Sanoma Syndication; 36 Dana Gallagher/Achard & Associates; 37 Gaelle le Boulicaut; 38 Dana Gallagher/Achard & Associates; 39 Margaret de Lange; 40 Christopher Drake/Red Cover; 41 Polly Wreford/Narratives; 42–3 Sally Chance/House and Leisure; 44 Marianne Luning/VT Wonen/Sanoma Syndication; 45 Polly Wreford/Narratives; 46 Solvi Dos Santos; 47 Tom Leighton/Elizabeth Whiting & Associates; 48–9 Jan Baldwin/Conran Octopus; 50 Di Lewis/Elizabeth Whiting & Associates; 51

James Merrell/Living Etc/IPC Syndication; 52 Courtesy of Sera of London; 52 above Courtesy of Amanda Ross; 53 Alex Sarginson; 54 Anson Smart; 55 Mark Williams/Living Etc/IPC Syndication; 56 Ray Main/Mainstream; 57 Martyn Thompson/Marie Claire Maison (Stylist: Marie Kalt); 58 Mel Yates (Designer: Sera of London); 59 Courtesy of Romo Fabrics; 60 Mel Yates/Elle Decoration; 61 Henry Bourne; 62 James Merrell/Living Etc/IPC Syndication; 63 Philippe Garcia/Marie Claire Maison (Stylist: Marion Bayle); 65 Tom Leighton/Living Etc/IPC Syndication; 66 above Courtesy of Osborne & Little; 66 below Courtesy of Neisha Crosland; 67 Edina Van Der Wyck/Homes & Gardens/IPC Syndication; 68 Mee, Bath (Artist: Kate Milson Hawkins); 68–9 Jacques Dirand/The Interior Archive (Designer: Carolyn Quartermaine); 70 Jake Curtis/Homes & Garden/IPC Syndication; 71 Tom Leighton/Living Etc/IPC Syndication; 72–5 Alexis Armanet/Marie Claire Maison (Stylist: Marion Bayle); 76–7 Courtesy of Timorous Beasties; 78 Adrian Briscoe (Lamp Designs by Plumo); 79 Bill Kingston/Elle Decoration; 80 above Courtesy of Neisha Crosland; 80 below Courtesy of Cath Kidston Ltd; 81 Graham Atkins-Hughes/Elle Decoration; 82 Bill Kingston/Elle Decoration; 83 David Hiscock/Homes & Gardens/IPC Syndication; 84 above Graham Atkins-Hughes/Elle Decoration; 84–5 Lina Ikse Bergman/Elle Decoration; 86 Graham Atkins-Hughes/Elle Decoration; 87 Mathew Shave/Elle Decoration; 88 Mel Yates/Elle Decoration; 89 Bill Kingston/Elle Decoration; 90 Chris Tubbs/Elle Decoration; 91 Mel Yates/Elle Decoration; 92 Jake Fitzjones/Living Etc/IPC Syndication; 93 Mel Yates/Elle Decoration; 94 above Courtesy of Osborne & Little; 94 below Courtesy

of Rachel Kelly; 95 Chris Tubbs; 96 Paul Massey/Living Etc/IPC Syndication; 97 above Courtesy of Missoni Home; 97 below Mai-Linh/Marie Claire Maison; 98 Courtesy of The Rug Company (Design by Lulu Guinness); 99 Courtesy of The Rug Company (Design by Diane von Furstenberg); 100 Adrian Briscoe/Elle Decoration; 101 Courtesy of Habitat UK; 102–3 Craig Knowles/Elle Decoration; 104–5 Courtesy of Svenskt Tenn; 106 Thomas Stewart/Elle Decoration; 107 Mel Yates/Elle Decoration; 108 above Courtesy of Tapettitalo; 108 below Courtesy of Osborne & Little; 109 Jan Baldwin/Narratives; 110 Annika Vannerus; 111–12 Jan Baldwin/Narratives; 113 Pia Tyler/Living Etc/IPC Syndication; 114 Dennis Brandsma/VT Wonen/Sanoma Syndication; 115 Chris Tubbs/Conran Octopus; 116 below Courtesy of Tapettitalo; 117 Wilfried Overwater/Taverne Agency (Stylist: Rosa Lisa); 118 Simon Brown/Red Cover; 119 Ulrike Schade/Elle Decoration; 120 Graham Atkins-Hughes; 121 Mel Yates/Elle Decoration; 122–3 David Woolley; 124–5 Courtesy of Cabbages and Roses; 126 Torsten Oelscher/Elle Decoration; 128 above Courtesy of Cabbages and Roses; 128 below Courtesy of Anna French; 129 Polly Wreford/Homes & Gardens/IPC Syndication; 130 Craig Fordham/Homes & Gardens/IPC Syndication; 131 Margaret de Lange; 132 Stuart McIntyre (Stylist: Lene Utzon); 133 Alexander Van Berge/Taverne Agency/Elle Eten; 134 Lisa Cohen/Vogue Living; 135 Tim Beddow/The Interior Archive (Designer: VV Rouleaux); 136–7 James Merrell/Homes & Gardens/IPC Syndication; 138 Yutaka Yamamoto/Marie Claire Maison; 139 Sally Chance/House and Leisure; 140–1 Andrew Wood/The Interior Archive; 142 Courtesy of Cath Kidston Ltd; 143 Margaret de Lange; 144 Jan Baldwin/Narratives; 145 Niels Harving/Lykke

Foged; 146 Studio Dreyer Hensley (Stylist: Paul Lowe); 147 Gaelle le Boulicaut; 148 Margaret de Lange; 150–1 Edina Van der Wyck/The Interior Archive; 152 Pia Tryde/Homes & Gardens/IPC Syndication; 153 Edina van der Wyck/The Interior Archive; 154 Edina van der Wyck/Courtesy of Cabbages and Roses; 155 Mark Broussard/Homes & Gardens/IPC Syndication

Every effort has been made to trace the copyright holders. We apologize in advance for unintentional omissions and would be pleased to insert the appropriate acknowledgment in any subsequent publication.

FABRIC AND WALLPAPER SWATCHES
10 Cath Kidston Petals; 14t Cath Kidston Bleached Rose Paisley (blue); 14b Curtain Exchange; 34t Cath Kidston Rose Stripe; 34b Cabbages & Roses Cerise Hatley; 48 De Gournay wallpaper; 52t Amanda Ross; 52b Sera of London Aroused Rose wallpaper (copper & gold rose on black); 59 Romo fabrics Japonica; 66t Osborne & Little Papilio wallpaper; 66b Neisha Crosland Merlin Plough Green; 76 Timorous Beasties McGegan Rose; 80t Neisha Crosland Tudor Plum Rose; 80b Cath Kidston Ottoman Rose (blue); 94t Osborne & Little Sakura collection Asuka design; 94b Rachel Kelly; 97t Missoni Home Ester; 97b Cacharel; 104 Svenskt Tenn Milles Fleurs (designed by Josef Frank); 108t Tapettitalo; 108b Osborne & Little Adelphi collection Tamara design; 116t Liberty; 116b Tapettitalo; 124 Cabbages & Roses Bees; 128t Cabbages & Roses Blue Podge; 128b Anna French Bird in the Bush; 142t Cath Kidston Bleached Summer Blossom; 142b Cath Kidston Antique Rose.